BLOCKBUSTERS GOLD RUN Volume 2

This book adaptation of *Blockbusters* 'Gold Run'
can be used in two ways. By yourself you can
solve the clues as you would a crossword puzzle,
writing the answers in the spaces provided and
shading or colouring in the hexagons; or, you can
play it as a game with a friend, one being the
quizmaster, and one being the competitor, trying
to get a link from left to right across the board in
sixty seconds – or however long you feel is fair.

Whether you solve the clues yourself, or with a
friend, you'll have hours of amusement and have
masses of information at your fingertips.

Blockbusters
Gold Run
Volume 2

**Based on the Central Independent Television
series produced in association with Mark
Goodson and Talbot Television Ltd**

SPHERE BOOKS LIMITED

First published in Great Britain by
Sphere Books Ltd 1987
27 Wrights Lane, London W8 5TZ
Copywright © 1987 by Sphere Books Ltd
Central logo copyright © 1982
Central Independent Television plc.
Central television programmes © 1983, 1984, 1985, 1986, 1987
Central Independent Television plc.

Blockbusters Gold Run questions compiled by Elizabeth
Comstock-Smith

Sphere Books claim full responsibility for the questions and
answers in this volume and every effort has been made to
ensure their accuracy.

TRADE
MARK

Set in Times

Printed and bound in Great Britain by
Richard Clay Ltd, Bungay, Suffolk

Blockbusters
Gold Run
Volume 2

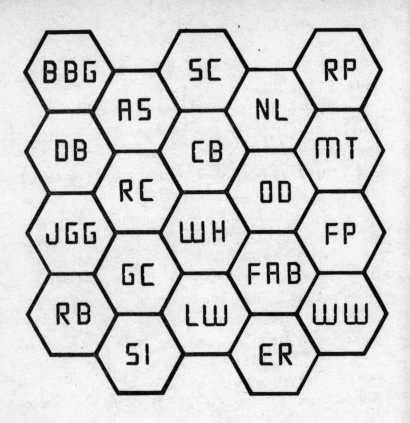

BBG	------------------	WH	------------------
DB	------------------	LW	------------------
JGG	------------------	NL	------------------
RB	------------------	OD	------------------
AS	------------------	FAB	------------------
RC	------------------	ER	------------------
GC	------------------	RP	------------------
SI	------------------	MT	------------------
SC	------------------	FP	------------------
CB	------------------	WW	------------------

BBG: Which 'BBG' plays JR's mother?

DB: Which 'DB' sang with The Spiders From Mars?

JGG: Which 'JGG' advertises tinned sweetcorn?

RB: Which 'RB' wrote *When the Wind Blows*?

AS: What 'AS' lies between Greece and Asia Minor?

RC: What 'RC' is money that bounces?

GC: What 'GC' governs the treatment of prisoners of war?

SI: Which 'SI' means looking exactly like someone else – possibly a rubber puppet?

SC: What 'SC' contains Michelangelo's *Last Judgement*?

CB: What 'CB' means permission to buy anything?

WH: Which 'WH' was the first Viceroy of India?

LW: What 'LW' is danced and sung in the musical *Me and My Girl*?

NL: What 'NL' does a lucky cat have?

OD: What 'OD' was built in 785 A.D. as a boundary between Wales and Mercia?

FAB: What 'FAB' is your family – what are they made of?

ER: What 'ER' starred Peter Fonda and Dennis Hopper as motorcyclists?

RP: What 'RP' was the notorious home of the mass-murderer Christie?

MT: What 'MT' is the day before Good Friday?

FP: Which 'FP' was the tennis star whose statue was unveiled at Wimbledon in 1984?

WW: What 'WW' was the land of the cowboys?

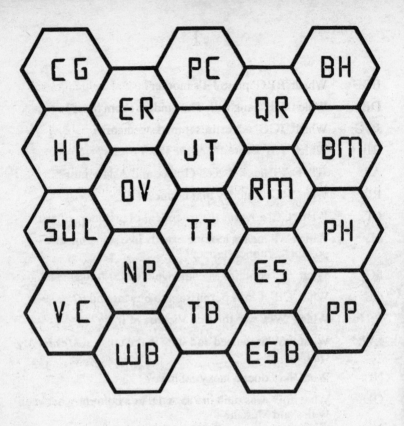

CG	-------------------	TT	-------------------
HC	-------------------	TB	-------------------
SUL	-------------------	QR	-------------------
VC	-------------------	RM	-------------------
ER	-------------------	ES	-------------------
OV	-------------------	ESB	-------------------
NP	-------------------	BH	-------------------
WB	-------------------	BM	-------------------
PC	-------------------	PH	-------------------
JT	-------------------	PP	-------------------

CG: What 'CG's did the Beach Boys wish all women were?

HC: What 'HC' was observed in 1683 and also in 1986?

SUL: What 'SUL' is meant to be a facial characteristic of traditional Englishmen?

VC: What 'VC' in Rome has its own stamps?

ER: Which 'ER' produces a guide to British hotels and restaurants every year?

OV: What 'OV' was the original home of the National Theatre?

NP: What 'NP' was first reached by Robert Peary in 1909?

WB: What 'WB' means a spoilsport – possibly damp?

PC: What 'PC' was the scene of Richard II's murder?

JT: Which 'JT's paintings are to have a new home of their own at the Tate Gallery?

TT: Which 'TT' was once married to Ike and has recently made a successful come-back?

TB: What 'TB' is an illegitimate child born the wrong side of?

QR: What 'QR's are a code of fighting for boxers?

RM: What 'RM' is chairman of Oxford Football Club and the Mirror Group?

ES: Which 'ES' illustrated *Winnie the Pooh*?

ESB: What 'ESB' was for a long time the tallest building in New York?

BH: Which 'BH' did Bing Crosby star with in the 'Road' movies?

BM: What 'BM' is where you buy illegal or unobtainable goods?

PH: What 'PH' brought America into World War II?

PP: Which 'PP' was a *Coronation Street* star who died in 1986?

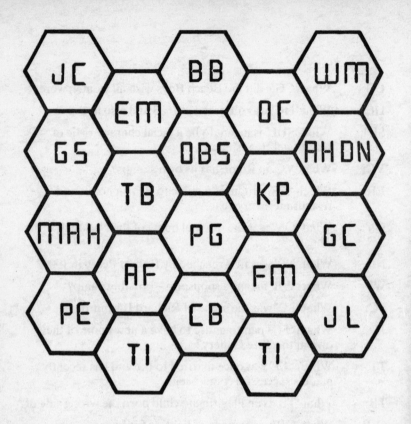

JC	-------------------	PG	-------------------
GS	-------------------	CB	-------------------
MAH	-------------------	OC	-------------------
PE	-------------------	KP	-------------------
EM	-------------------	FM	-------------------
TB	-------------------	TI	-------------------
AF	-------------------	WM	-------------------
TI	-------------------	AHDN	-------------------
BB	-------------------	GC	-------------------
OBS	-------------------	JL	-------------------

JC: Which 'JC' says, 'You dirty rat' in gangster movies?

GS: What 'GS' brought Britain to a standstill in 1926?

MAH: What 'MAH' did Moses say would flow in the land of Israel?

PE: What 'PE' means the birth-rate has gone up dramatically?

EM: What 'EM's were brought to England from Greece in 1812 and are now, controversially, in the British Museum?

TB: What 'TB's are the sign over a pawnbroker's shop?

AF: Which 'AF' recorded 'Women Are Doing It For Themselves' with Annie Lennox?

TI: What 'TI' means 'unknown land' on ancient maps?

BB: What 'BB' happened to the Stock Exchange in October 1986?

OBS: What 'OBS's train adventurous teenagers?

PG: Which 'PG' is famous for his paintings of Hawaiian natives?

CB: Which 'CB's dog is called Snoopy?

OC: What 'OC' was the nickname of the British Expeditionary Force in 1914?

KP: What 'KP' was originally called Nottingham House?

FM: Which 'FM' is a television and radio personality famous for his lisp, moustache and bow-tie?

TI: What 'TI' starred Paul Newman, Steve McQueen and Fred Astaire and was a raging success?

WM: Which 'WM' was a leading member of the Pre-Raphaelite Movement?

AHDN: Which 'AHDN' starred the Beatles and featured the song 'Can't Buy Me Love'?

GC: What 'GC' is in Arizona and rather deep?

JL: Which 'JL' was the boxer known as the 'Brown Bomber'?

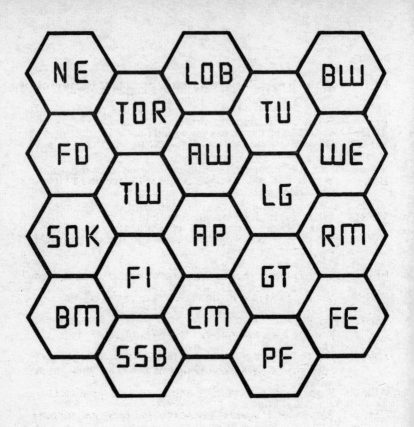

NE	-------------------	AP	-------------------
FD	-------------------	CM	-------------------
SOK	-------------------	TU	-------------------
BM	-------------------	LG	-------------------
TOR	-------------------	GT	-------------------
TW	-------------------	PF	-------------------
FI	-------------------	BW	-------------------
SSB	-------------------	WE	-------------------
LOB	-------------------	RM	-------------------
AW	-------------------	FE	-------------------

NE: Which 'NE's TV show was stopped in 1986 because of an accidental death on the programme?

FD: What 'FD' is time; the first three being space?

SOK: What 'SOK' do fans call horse racing – perhaps particularly the royal family?

BM: Which 'BM' was a reggae singer who received a UN Peace Medal?

TOR: What 'TOR' did Einstein publish in 1906?

TW: Which 'TW' is the Archbishop of Canterbury's Special Envoy?

FI: What 'FI' is part of the Shetlands famous for its knitting?

SSB: What 'SSB' is the National Anthem of the USA?

LOB: What 'LOB' starred the Monty Python team and was labelled blasphemous by Mary Whitehouse?

AW: Which 'AW' is an American pop artist famous for his paintings of Campbell's soup tins and Marilyn Monroe?

AP: From what 'AP' was BBC television first broadcast?

CM: What 'CM' is a poverty-stricken, but religious, rodent?

TU: What 'TU's represent workers?

LG: Which 'LG' plays Dirty Den in *East Enders*?

GT: What 'GT' is where many of Shakespeare's plays were originally performed?

PF: Which 'PF's were Puritans who emigrated to America?

BW: Which 'BW' had a servant called Jeeves?

WE: What 'WE' is something very large nobody wants – possibly with a long nose and sold on a stall?

RM: What 'RM' runs a certain distance in Edinburgh, starting at Holyrood Castle?

FE: What 'FE' is a name for the reign of Napoleon I?

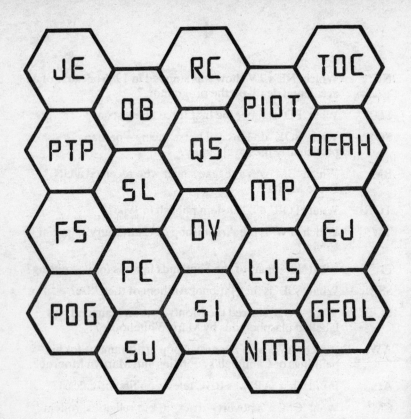

JE	------------------	DV	------------------
PTP	------------------	SI	------------------
FS	------------------	PIOT	------------------
POG	------------------	MP	------------------
OB	------------------	LJS	------------------
SL	------------------	NMA	------------------
PC	------------------	TOC	------------------
SJ	------------------	OFAH	------------------
RC	------------------	EJ	------------------
QS	------------------	GFOL	------------------

JE: Which 'JE' married her employer, Mr Rochester?

PTP: What 'PTP' is from one end of the world to the other?

FS: What 'FS' is the home of many of England's newspapers?

POG: What 'POG' do you find at the end of the rainbow?

OB: What 'OB' is the site of the Central Criminal Courts in London?

SL: What 'SL' is the oldest classic horse race in Britain?

PC: What 'PC's are red, yellow and blue?

SJ: What 'SJ' is part of the ring road round Birmingham?

RC: What 'RC' was the armistice ending World War I signed in?

QS: What 'QS' is the road you live on when you have no money left?

DV: Which 'DV' was Luke Skywalker's father?

SI: What 'SI' is the grammatical error in 'to boldly go'?

PIOT: What 'PIOT' did Chamberlain promise on his return from Munich in 1938?

MP: Which 'MP' loves Kermit the Frog?

LJS: Which 'LJS' had a wooden leg and a parrot?

NMA: What 'NMA' was the fighting force raised by Oliver Cromwell?

TOC: What 'TOC' is the lowest card in the pack?

OFAH: What 'OFAH' features Del Boy and Rodney?

EJ: Which 'EJ' is a rock star whose real name is Reginald Dwight?

GFOL: What 'GFOL' broke out in Pudding Lane in 1666?

GI	-------------------	RC	-------------------
RC	-------------------	CP	-------------------
MC	-------------------	GR	-------------------
BP	-------------------	MG	-------------------
KE	-------------------	YAY	-------------------
TBO	-------------------	PMF	-------------------
CR	-------------------	JL	-------------------
BB	-------------------	NBN	-------------------
GT	-------------------	MG	-------------------
BK	-------------------	GG	-------------------

GI: What 'GI's were visited by Darwin and written about by him because of their extraordinary wild-life?

RC: What 'RC' is a golf tournament played between the USA and Europe?

MC: Which 'MC' discovered radium?

BP: What 'BP' is one of Picasso's most famous series of early paintings?

KE: What 'KE' is another, royal, name for scrofula?

TBO: What 'TBO' was a medieval way of establishing guilt or innocence?

CR: What 'CR' does your money go into in a shop?

BB: Which 'BB's made a musical film in which they were 'on a mission from God'?

GT: What 'GT' is a deserted conurbation, usually in America?

BK: What 'BK' go 'aaah' at the smell of gravy?

RC: Which 'RC' wrote detective stories about Philip Marlowe?

CP: What 'CP's are Dover, Hastings, Hythe, Romney and Sandwich?

GR: What 'GR' sent people looking for wealth in California in 1848?

MG: Which 'MG' is a festival you might go to New Orleans to celebrate?

YAY: What 'YAY' is a basis of Chinese philosophy?

PMF: What 'PMF' means an extremely unlikely event – maybe something to do with the aerodynamics of pork?

JL: Which 'JL' is commemorated in the 1981 record by George Harrison, 'All Those Years Ago'?

NBN: What 'NBN' was directed by Hitchcock and starred Cary Grant on Mount Rushmore?

MG: Which 'MG' was a pop singer shot dead by his father in 1984?

GG: Which 'GG' shouldn't you kill if you want to continue getting valuable eggs?

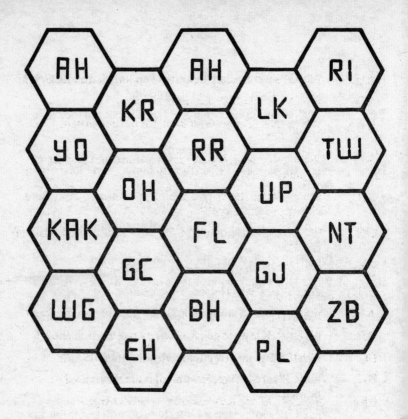

AH	-----------------	FL	-----------------
YO	-----------------	BH	-----------------
KAK	-----------------	LK	-----------------
WG	-----------------	UP	-----------------
KR	-----------------	GJ	-----------------
OH	-----------------	PL	-----------------
GC	-----------------	RI	-----------------
EH	-----------------	TW	-----------------
AH	-----------------	NT	-----------------
RR	-----------------	ZB	-----------------

AH: Which 'AH' starred Woody Allen and Diane Keaton?

YO: Which 'YO' is John Lennon's widow?

KAK: Which 'KAK' are you related to, particularly in Scotland?

WG: What 'WG' was Robert Graves' muse and perfect woman?

KR: What 'KR' is the large amount of money you pay for a kidnapped monarch?

OH: What 'OH' was bought by Queen Victoria on the Isle of Wight?

GC: What 'GC' honours bravery by civilians?

EH: Which 'EH' was Nelson's mistress?

AH: What 'AH' is a vulnerable spot – possibly on the foot?

RR: What 'RR' is a rodent with his own television show?

FL: What 'FL' is an army joined by desperate men?

BH: What 'BH' is a film famous for its chariot race?

LK: Which 'LK' wanted *you* during World War I?

UP: What 'UP' is a major art gallery in Florence?

GJ: Which 'GJ' made a recent recording of 'La Vie En Rose'?

PL: What 'PL' is Ted Hughes?

RI: Which 'RI' gave up editorship of *Private Eye* in 1986?

TW: What 'TW' do you pour oil on in order to calm things down?

NT: What 'NT' was Welwyn Garden City the first example of?

ZB: Which 'ZB' trained with her pet springbok?

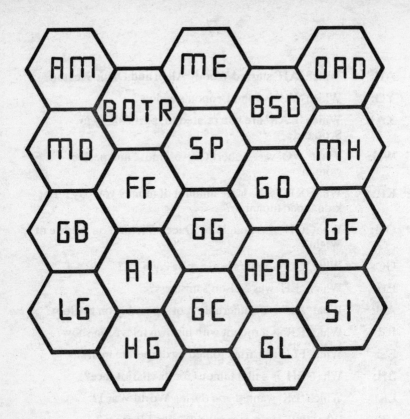

AM	-----------------	GG	-----------------
MD	-----------------	GC	-----------------
GB	-----------------	BSD	-----------------
LG	-----------------	GO	-----------------
BOTR	-----------------	AFOD	-----------------
FF	-----------------	GL	-----------------
AI	-----------------	OAD	-----------------
HG	-----------------	MH	-----------------
ME	-----------------	GF	-----------------
SP	-----------------	SI	-----------------

AM: Which 'AM' wrote his secret diary at the age of thirteen and three-quarters?

MD: Which 'MD' collided with Zola Budd in the 1984 Olympics?

GB: What 'GB' is the protected countryside around a city or town?

LG: What 'LG' is another name for the *Mona Lisa*?

BOTR: What 'BOTR' had an album cover featuring Michael Parkinson, Clement Freud, Christopher Lee, John Conteh and Linda McCartney?

FF: What 'FF' is tempting but not allowed, particularly in Eden?

AI: What 'AI' fights for the rights of political prisoners?

HG: What 'HG' were *Dad's Army* part of?

ME: What 'ME' was climbed by Hillary and Tensing in 1953?

SP: What 'SP' won't fit into a round hole?

GG: What 'GG' do you elope to?

GC: What 'GC' measures radio-activity?

BSD: What 'BSD' don't you want sitting behind you in a car?

GO: What 'GO' was built on the banks of the Thames by Sir Christopher Wren?

AFOD: What 'AFOD' was Clint Eastwood's first major film?

GL: What 'GL' is a sign to go ahead?

OAD: What 'OAD' commemorates the Restoration of Charles II?

MH: What 'MH' is the official residence of the Lord Mayor of London?

GF: What 'GF' is an operatic season held annually in Sussex?

SI: What 'SI' was another name for Hawaii?

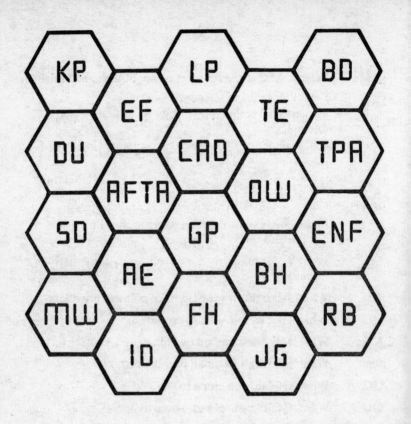

KP	--------------------	GP	--------------------
DU	--------------------	FH	--------------------
SD	--------------------	TE	--------------------
MW	--------------------	OW	--------------------
EF	--------------------	BH	--------------------
AFTA	--------------------	JG	--------------------
AE	--------------------	BD	--------------------
ID	--------------------	TPA	--------------------
LP	--------------------	ENF	--------------------
CAD	--------------------	RB	--------------------

KP: What 'KP' lies between Pakistan and Afghanistan?

DU: What 'DU' is slang for Australia?

SD: Which 'SD' is a leading Spanish surrealist painter?

MW: Which 'MW's catchphrase was, 'Come up and see me sometime'?

EF: Which 'EF' is a television soap opera about rural folk?

AFTA: What 'AFTA' is a novel by Ernest Hemingway?

AE: What 'AE' is your opposite personality?

ID: What 'ID' is the fourth of July?

LP: What 'LP' is the name given to the sitting of the House of Commons forcibly broken up by Oliver Cromwell?

CAD: Which 'CAD' are a cockney singing duo?

GP: What 'GP' is a means of finding people's opinions – usually in the street?

FH: What 'FH' will announce the Apocalypse?

TE: Which 'TE's designed Lady Diana's wedding dress?

OW: What 'OW' was the name of the conflict between China and England in the 19th century?

BH: Which 'BH' was a rock star killed in a plane crash in 1959?

JG: Which 'JG' is the sports presenter who used to play for Chelsea, Tottenham and West Ham?

BD: What 'BD' is the last bit of American money you make a sure bet with?

TPA: From what 'TPA' was a lot of American jazz meant to have come?

ENF: What 'ENF' are pachyderms who remember everything?

RB: Which 'RB' sang the song and starred in the film *Camelot*?

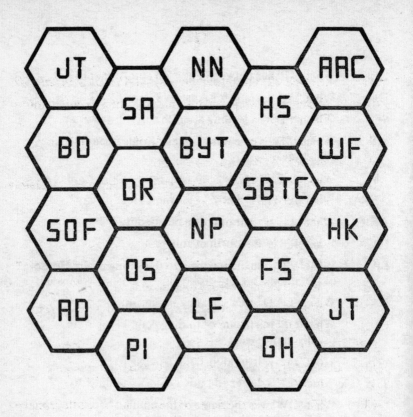

JT	-------------------	NP	-------------------
BD	-------------------	LF	-------------------
SOF	-------------------	HS	-------------------
AD	-------------------	SBTC	-------------------
SA	-------------------	FS	-------------------
DR	-------------------	GH	-------------------
OS	-------------------	AAC	-------------------
PI	-------------------	WF	-------------------
NN	-------------------	HK	-------------------
BYT	-------------------	JT	-------------------

JT: Which 'JT' illustrated the original *Alice in Wonderland*?

BD: What 'BD' is a piece of furniture a girl is meant to fill before her wedding?

SOF: What 'SOF' is another name for the Quakers?

AD: Which 'AD' presents TV-AM?

SA: What 'SA' is the London tennis tournament immediately before Wimbledon?

DR: Which 'DR' wrote *Guys and Dolls*?

OS: What 'OS' is a detailed kind of map?

PI: What 'PI' was colonised by mutineers from the *Bounty*?

NN: What 'NN' do you pay on with hire purchase?

BYT: What 'BYT' were people of the 1920s described as in *Brideshead Revisited*?

NP: What 'NP' was founded by the inventor of dynamite?

LF: What 'LF' can a clever manipulator twist someone round?

HS: What 'HS' was Emperor of Ethiopia and spiritual leader of the Rastafarians?

SBTC: What 'SBTC' takes a long time to sail to the Far East?

FS: Which 'FS' is known as Old Blue Eyes?

GH: Which 'GH' is Lofty's full name in *East Enders*?

AAC: Which 'AAC' met amongst others, Frankenstein; the Invisible Man; Dr Jekyll and Mr Hyde; the Keystone Cops?

WF: What 'WF' is a sign of surrender?

HK: What 'HK' is ritual Japanese suicide?

JT: Which 'JT' is famous for his depressed cartoon dogs?

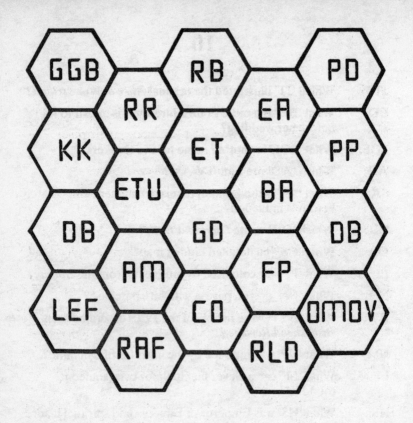

GCB	-----------------	GD	-----------------
KK	-----------------	CO	-----------------
DB	-----------------	EA	-----------------
LEF	-----------------	BA	-----------------
RR	-----------------	FP	-----------------
ETU	-----------------	RLD	-----------------
AM	-----------------	PD	-----------------
RAF	-----------------	PP	-----------------
RB	-----------------	DB	-----------------
ET	-----------------	OMOV	-----------------

GGB: What 'GGB' is San Francisco's most famous landmark?

KK: Which 'KK' was the Emperor who built Xanadu?

DB: What 'DB' is the lowest-pitched member of the violin family?

LEF: What 'LEF' is the motto of Republican France?

RR: What 'RR' does one have to get out of in order to live a peaceful life?

ETU: Which 'ETU' ruled England from 978–1016 AD?

AM: What 'AM's are lithium, sodium, potassium, rubidium and caesium?

RAF: What 'RAF' is the non-commissioned majority of the army?

RB: Which 'RB' broke the four minute mile in 1954?

ET: What 'ET' is the consortium which will one day link the UK and France?

GD: What 'GD' is a central ritual in the Red Indian religion – rather a spooky one?

CO: What 'CO's include, Doctor; Up the Khyber; Camping and Screaming?

EA: What 'EA' was the site of Montgomery's victory over Rommel?

BA: What 'BA' is the only monkey native to Europe and is particularly found on Gibraltar?

FP: What 'FP' is caused by salmonella bacteria?

RLD: What 'RLD' is a special event on the calendar?

PD: Which 'PD' presents *Every Second Counts*?

PP: What 'PP' is someone who ruins a celebration?

DB: What 'DB' is a large area of sand in the North Sea off Northumberland?

OMOV: What 'OMOV' is the motto of democracy and its basic principle?

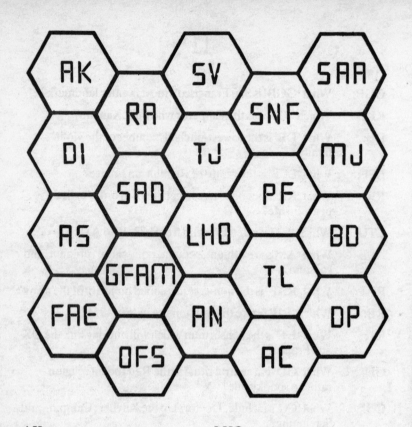

AK	------------------	LHO	------------------
DI	------------------	AN	------------------
AS	------------------	SNF	------------------
FAE	------------------	PF	------------------
RA	------------------	TL	------------------
SAD	------------------	AC	------------------
GFAM	------------------	SAA	------------------
OFS	------------------	MJ	------------------
SV	------------------	BD	------------------
TJ	------------------	DP	------------------

AK: Which 'AK' is the current religious and political leader of the Persians?

DI: What 'DI' was a notorious penal colony off the coast of South America?

AS: What 'AS' is rain we expect in the Spring?

FAE: What 'FAE' is a Jeffrey Archer novel about parliamentary candidates?

RA: Which 'RA' lost his job as manager of Manchester United in 1986?

SAD: What 'SAD' did highwaymen demand of their victims?

GFAM: What 'GFAM' did the three kings bring as gifts?

OFS: What 'OFS' is a province of South Africa?

SV: What 'SV' is a high-tech area of California?

TJ: What 'TJ' do motorists hate getting into – it may be sticky?

LHO: Which 'LHO' shot President John Kennedy?

AN: What 'AN' means an alias?

SNF: What 'SNF' was the film that brought together John Travolta and the Bee Gees?

PF: What 'PF' is a flooded area in which rice is cultivated?

TL: What 'TL' is cockney slang for a thief?

AC: What 'AC' is the major organ in our bodies that deals with digestion?

SAA: What 'SAA' is worn, particularly in the Bible, to show deep repentance and grief?

MJ: Which 'MJ' is the pop star who played the part of Ned Kelly?

BD: What 'BD' is presented by Cilla Black?

DP: What 'DP' is a large dog, often used in police or guard work?

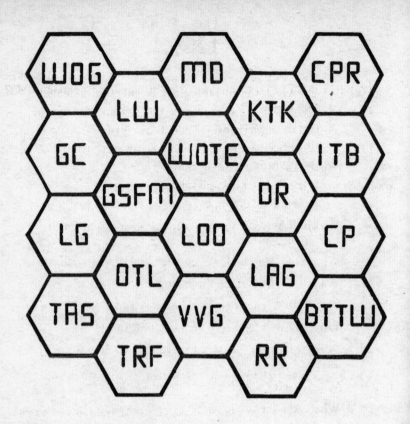

WOG	-----------------	LOO	-----------------
GC	-----------------	VVG	-----------------
LG	-----------------	KTK	-----------------
TAS	-----------------	DR	-----------------
LW	-----------------	LAG	-----------------
GSFM	-----------------	RR	-----------------
OTL	-----------------	CPR	-----------------
TRF	-----------------	ITB	-----------------
MD	-----------------	CP	-----------------
WOTE	-----------------	BTTW	-----------------

WOG: What 'WOG' will take place in Calgary, Canada in 1988?

GC: What 'GC' is a rocky headland on the north coast of Northern Ireland?

LG: What 'LG' is the common name for nitrous oxide, sometimes used as an anaesthetic in dentistry?

TAS: What 'TAS' is cockney slang for a wife?

LW: Which 'LW' was turned into a pillar of salt?

GSFM: What 'GSFM' did Neil Armstrong make in 1969?

OTL: What 'OTL' mustn't you be if you are driving a car?

TRF: What 'TRF' is the anthem of socialism?

MD: What 'MD' was the great white whale?

WOTE: What 'WOTE' should a soldier see before shooting the enemy?

LOO: What 'LOO' is America described as by immigrants?

VVG: Which 'VVG' was a Dutch painter who committed suicide?

KTK: Which 'KTK' sang at Prince Charles and Lady Diana's wedding?

DR: What 'DR' is a doctrine supporting hereditary kingship and was claimed by James I and Charles I?

LAG: What 'LAG' is Friday's child?

RR: Which 'RR' was the film actor who nearly starred in *Casablanca* instead of Humphrey Bogart?

CPR: What 'CPR' linked the Pacific and Atlantic Oceans when completed in 1885?

ITB: What 'ITB' are the first words of the Bible?

CP: What 'CP' is associated with a hare lip?

BTTW: What 'BTTW' means one is in a desperate situation – there is no escape behind you?

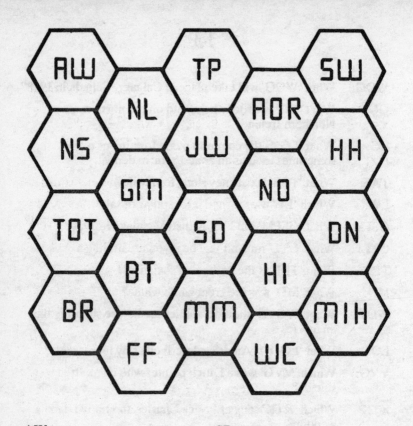

AW	------------------	SD	------------------
NS	------------------	MM	------------------
TOT	------------------	AOR	------------------
BR	------------------	NO	------------------
NL	------------------	HI	------------------
GM	------------------	WC	------------------
BT	------------------	SW	------------------
FF	------------------	HH	------------------
TP	------------------	DN	------------------
JW	------------------	MIH	------------------

AW: What 'AW' is a short time in politics according to Harold Wilson?

NS: What 'NS' is a province of Canada whose capital is Halifax?

TOT: What 'TOT' do children do on Halloween?

BR: What 'BR' takes place on the Thames between Oxford and Cambridge?

NL: What 'NL' do you turn over in order to make a fresh start?

GM: What 'GM' is a venomous lizard found in South West America and Mexico?

BT: What 'BT's does one come down to when discussing a basic issue?

FF: What 'FF' was owed to the bells of St Martin's?

TP: What 'TP' houses the US Department of Defence?

JW: Which 'JW' was the tough guy whose real name was Marion Michael Morrison?

SD: Which 'SD' is a snooker star who appeared at a Conservative Party rally?

MM: What 'MM' is a reminder of death?

AOR: What 'AOR' took place in the 18th century and was also known as the Enlightenment?

NO: What 'NO' is the aristocracy's duty, particularly in France?

HI: What 'HI' is Mrs Arthur Daley known as in *Minder*?

WC: What 'WC', demolished in 1984, was the home of Queens Park Rangers?

SW: What 'SW's proverbially run deep?

HH: Which 'HH' was the head of the Nazi SS from 1929–1945?

DN: What 'DN' is the common name for belladonna?

MIH: What 'MIH' do they say you repent at leisure?

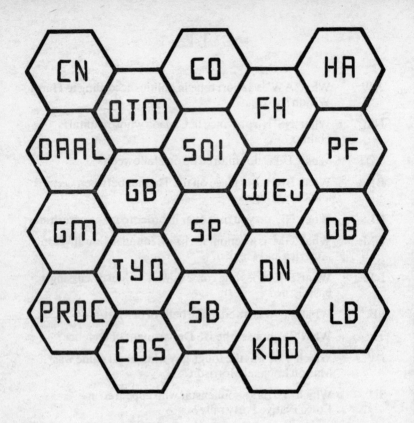

CN	------------------	SP	------------------
DAAL	------------------	SB	------------------
GM	------------------	FH	------------------
PROC	------------------	WEJ	------------------
OTM	------------------	DN	------------------
GB	------------------	KOD	------------------
TYO	------------------	HA	------------------
CDS	------------------	PF	------------------
CO	------------------	DB	------------------
SOI	------------------	LB	------------------

CN: What 'CN's stand on the Embankment and in Central Park, New York?

DAAL: What 'DAAL' means as inebriated as a titled man?

GM: Which 'GM' was an American band-leader who disappeared over the Channel during World War II?

PROC: What 'PROC' is the most populous country in the world?

OTM: What 'OTM' is a phrase we are told happy football managers use (or possibly astronauts)?

GB: What 'GB' stores bile from the liver?

TYO: What 'TYO' starred Rick Mayall, Ade Edmonson and Alexi Sayle?

CDS: What 'CDS' is a dead end in French?

CO: What 'CO' was the average man in London meant to travel on?

SOI: Which 'SOI' was deposed from the Peacock Throne in 1979?

SP: What 'SP' is a tough, shaggy animal associated with the far north of Scotland?

SB: Which 'SB' is wife of Andrew Lloyd Webber and star of his latest musicals?

FH: What 'FH' is a pub not owned by a particular brewery?

WEJ: Which 'WEJ' wrote the Biggles books?

DN: What 'DN' was the first James Bond film?

KOD: What 'KOD' means a fatal embrace?

HA: What 'HA' is associated with coronary thrombosis?

PF: What 'PF' is needed if two horses end a race neck and neck?

DB: What 'DB' was a national survey made between 1085 and 1086?

LB: What 'LB' is falling down in the nursery rhyme?

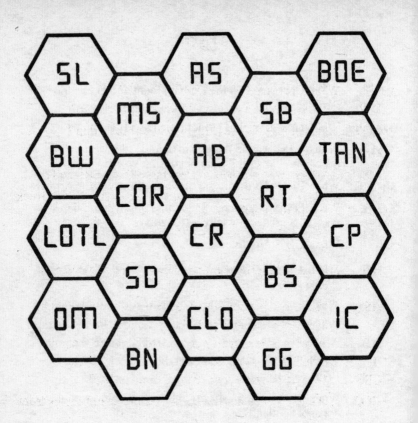

SL	------------------	CR	------------------
BW	------------------	CLO	------------------
LOTL	------------------	SB	------------------
OM	------------------	RT	------------------
MS	------------------	BS	------------------
COR	------------------	GG	------------------
SD	------------------	BOE	------------------
BN	------------------	TAN	------------------
AS	------------------	CP	------------------
AB	------------------	IC	------------------

SL: Which 'SL' is a member of Duran Duran?

BW: What 'BW' is a very rhythmic piano jazz style?

LOTL: Which 'LOTL' presented Excalibur to Arthur?

OM: What 'OM' is a spinster?

MS: Which 'MS' presents a Breakfast Show on Radio I?

COR: What 'COR' is a huge statue to Helio straddling a Greek Island harbour?

SD: What 'SD' is it too late to shut after the horse has bolted?

BN: What 'BN' is the wine raced to London in November every year?

AS: What 'AS' is a boy who doesn't leave home said to be attached to his mother by?

AB: What 'AB' is a display of coloured lights in the polar regions?

CR: What 'CR' was a spoof James Bond movie?

CLO. What 'CLO' is rich in vitamins A and D and comes from fish?

SB: Which 'SB' was the South American revolutionary leader known as the 'Liberator'?

RT: What 'RT' does excessive bureaucracy get wrapped up in?

BS: What 'BS' lies south-west of the USSR and north of Turkey?

GG: Which 'GG' wrote *The Female Eunuch*?

BOE: What 'BOE' is the Old Lady of Threadneedle Street?

TAN: What 'TAN' are parts of the body someone uses when they are fighting viciously and desperately?

CP: Which 'CP' was Henry VIII's widow?

IC: What 'IC' is said to divide East from West?

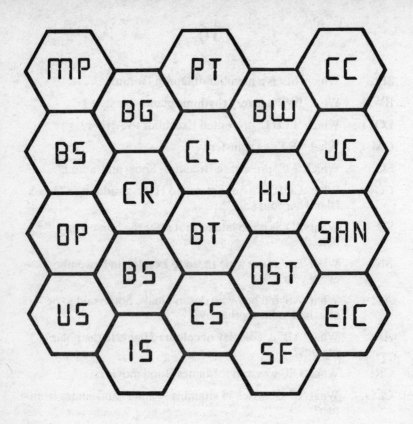

MP	------------------	BT	------------------
BS	------------------	CS	------------------
OP	------------------	BW	------------------
US	------------------	HJ	------------------
BG	------------------	OST	------------------
CR	------------------	SF	------------------
BS	------------------	CC	------------------
IS	------------------	JC	------------------
PT	------------------	SAN	------------------
CL	------------------	EIC	------------------

MP: Which 'MP' presents *Desert Island Discs*?

BS: Which 'BS' is a wastrel member of the family?

OP: What 'OP' produces a narcotic drug from which morphine and heroin are derived?

US: Which 'US' is meant to be the personification of America?

BG: Which 'BG's autobiography is called *Is That All*?

CR: What 'CR' killed the sparrow?

BS: What 'BS' drowned Leander and now provides access to the Black Sea?

IS: What 'IS' is a sunny and warm period of weather in the Autumn?

PT: Which 'PT' was leader of the Who and is now a publisher of books?

CL: What 'CL' is a juvenile adoration – possibly among cows?

BT: What 'BT' is the principal opera and ballet company in Moscow?

CS: What 'CS' is a small English dog with silky hair and drooping ears?

BW: What 'BW' is the largest known mammal?

HJ: Which 'HJ' played large parts in the 'Carry On' films?

OST: What 'OST' is meant to be a way of getting jobs through friends – worn around the neck by some men?

SF: What 'SF' is the political branch of the IRA?

CC: Which 'CC' wrote the 'Tilly Trotter' novels?

JC: What 'JC's are the places where cases involving children are tried?

SAN: What 'SAN' is the path to keep on in order to avoid temptation and wrongdoing?

EIC: What 'EIC' successfully introduced British trade into Bombay and other parts of Asia?

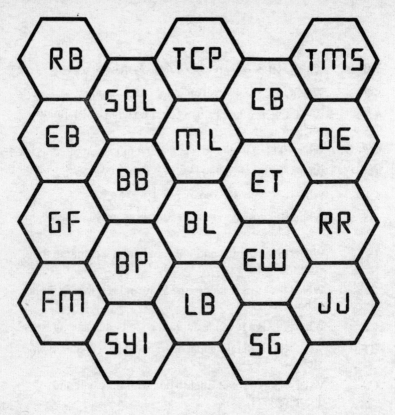

RB	------------------	BL	------------------
EB	------------------	LB	------------------
GF	------------------	CB	------------------
FM	------------------	ET	------------------
SOL	------------------	EW	------------------
BB	------------------	SG	------------------
BP	------------------	TMS	------------------
SYI	------------------	DE	------------------
TCP	------------------	RR	------------------
ML	------------------	JJ	------------------

RB: Which 'RB' is chairman of Virgin Records?

EB: What 'EB' gets the worm?

GF: What 'GF' did Jason and the Argonauts search for and find?

FM: Which 'FM' is lead singer of Queen?

SOL: Which 'SOL' celebrated her 100th birthday in 1986 in New York Harbor?

BB: Which 'BB' was the American showman William Cody known as?

BP: Which 'BP' immortalised a rabbit?

SYI: What 'SYI' are married men meant to get – a film starring Marilyn Monroe?

TCP: What 'TCP' was the story of a black woman, directed by Speilberg as a film of the same name and written by Alice Walker?

ML: What 'ML' is meant to join men to apes?

BL: What 'BL' contains a copy of every book published in the UK?

LB: Which 'LB' was said to have axed her mother and father to death in 1892?

CB: What 'CB' is broken by the last straw?

ET: What 'ET' was put up for the Paris Exhibition of 1889?

EW: Which 'EW' wrote *Put Out More Flags*, *Scoop* and *Black Mischief*?

SG: Which 'SG' was known as the most chivalrous of the knights of the Round Table?

TMS: What 'TMS' were led by Yul Brynner and based on a story about Samurai?

DE: What 'DE' measures the movements of heavenly objects?

RR: What 'RR' shouldn't you wave at a bull?

JJ: Which 'JJ' led a band of outlaws with his brother Frank?

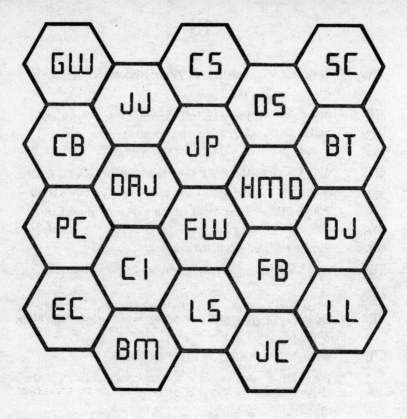

GW	----------------	FW	----------------
CB	----------------	LS	----------------
PC	----------------	DS	----------------
EC	----------------	HMD	----------------
JJ	----------------	FB	----------------
DAJ	----------------	JC	----------------
CI	----------------	SC	----------------
BM	----------------	BT	----------------
CS	----------------	DJ	----------------
JP	----------------	LL	----------------

GW: What 'GW's were Julius Caesar's military campaign in France?

CB: What 'CB' is also known as the clavicle?

PC: What 'PC' sang a duet with Sting at the Live Aid concert?

EC: What 'EC' suffered from insatiable curiosity?

JJ: What 'JJ' is a method of weaponless self-defence from which Judo is derived?

DAJ: What 'DAJ' are meant to be a typical elderly couple?

CI: What 'CI's are Jersey and Guernsey part of?

BM: What 'BM' is made with vodka and tomato juice?

CS: What 'CS' do you turn to someone you are ignoring?

JP: What 'JP' is a forward movement achieved by expanding gases ejected rearwards?

FW: Which 'FW' is a javelin thrower who was voted Sportswoman of the Year in 1986?

LS: What 'LS' are an animal's markings which are said never to change?

DS: What 'DS' lies below sea-level in Israel?

HMD: What 'HMD's are clothes passed to you, normally by an older brother or sister?

FB: What 'FB' was the film that originally featured Rambo?

JC: What 'JC' wrote *Hollywood Wives*, *Hollywood Husbands*, *Lucky*?

SC: What 'SC' swings low in a negro spiritual?

BT: What 'BT' was Buddha enlightened under?

DJ: Which 'DJ' was editor of the *Sun* and now presents a radio show?

LL: What 'LL' is an azure blue semi-precious gemstone?

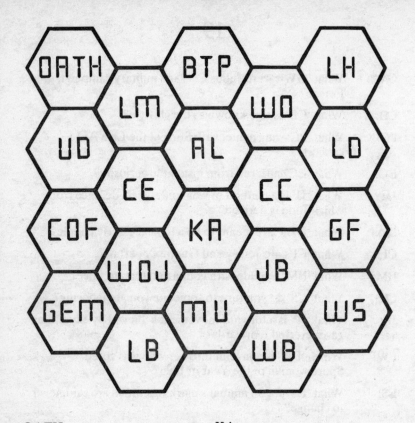

OATH	------------------	KA	------------------
UD	------------------	MU	------------------
COF	------------------	WO	------------------
GEM	------------------	CC	------------------
LM	------------------	JB	------------------
CE	------------------	WB	------------------
WOJ	------------------	LH	------------------
LB	------------------	LD	------------------
BTP	------------------	GF	------------------
AL	------------------	WS	------------------

OATH: What 'OATH' is a way of describing something ancient – maybe part of the landscape?

UD: What 'UD' became a swan?

COF: What 'COF' was David Putnam's first big success?

GEM: What 'GEM' is a description of jealousy – a horrible creature?

LM: What 'LM' sits in the harbour of Copenhagen, commemorating Hans Christian Andersen?

CE: What 'CE', eaten at breakfast, was good in parts?

WOJ: What 'WOJ' were brought down by Joshua?

LB: What 'LB's tail has the Pole Star at the end of it?

BTP: What 'BTP' is the incident meant to have sparked off the American Revolution?

AL: What 'AL' when rubbed should grant three wishes?

KA: Which 'KA' wrote *Lucky Jim* and won the Booker Prize in 1986?

MU: Which 'MU' is lead singer with Ultravox?

WO: What 'WO' is it a good idea to sow when you're young?

CC: What 'CC' is the most widespread human ailment?

JB: What 'JB' is the site of a large radio telescope in Cheshire?

WB: What 'WB' is another name for a scapegoat – a beaten youth?

LH: Which 'LH' beat Don Curry to win the undisputed world welterweight boxing crown in September 1986?

LD: Which 'LD' took over from Terry Wogan on *Blankety Blank*?

GF: What 'GF's is it useful for a gardener to have?

WS: What 'WS' is another name for the three witches in *Macbeth*?

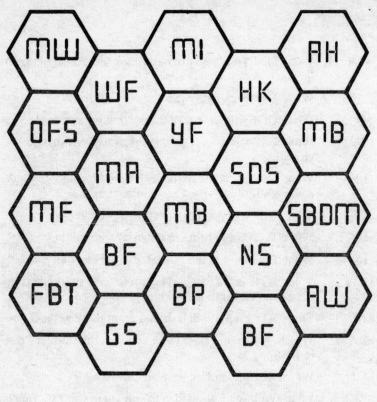

MW	------------------	MB	------------------
OFS	------------------	BP	------------------
MF	------------------	HK	------------------
FBT	------------------	SDS	------------------
WF	------------------	NS	------------------
MA	------------------	BF	------------------
BF	------------------	AH	------------------
GS	------------------	MB	------------------
MI	------------------	SBDM	------------------
YF	------------------	AW	------------------

MW: Which 'MW' presented *In Search of Troy* and *Domesday* on TV?

OFS: What 'OFS' is a single magpie meant to represent?

MF: What 'MF' is an American term for a knock-out drug?

FBT: What 'FBT' features Terry Hall and ex-members of the Specials?

WF: What 'WF' did women give to men they considered cowards in World War I?

MA: What 'MA' did Noah's Ark finally come to rest on?

BF: What 'BF' is a wooded region of West Germany famous for its gateaux?

GS: What 'GS' was a person condemned to row a Roman ship?

MI: Which 'MI' is the production team that brought us *A Room With A View* and *Shakespeare Wallah*?

YF: What 'YF' does a ship run up to show it is in quarantine?

MB: Which 'MB' was the famous manager of Manchester United who was knighted in 1968?

BP: What 'BP' wouldn't you touch someone with if you distrusted or disliked them?

HK: Which 'HK' was West German Chancellor in 1986?

SDS: What 'SDS' include gluttony, lust and sloth?

NS: Which 'NS' wrote *A Town Like Alice*?

BF: What 'BF' is made with champagne and orange juice – also the name of a pop group?

AH: Which 'AH' was reputed to be Shakespeare's wife?

MB: What 'MB' is an oval-shaped hand-grenade?

SBDM: What 'SBDM' is the name of the slaughter of French Huguenots in 1572?

AW: What 'AW' relies on hydrostatic pressure to force water to the surface – there are lots of them in the Australian outback?

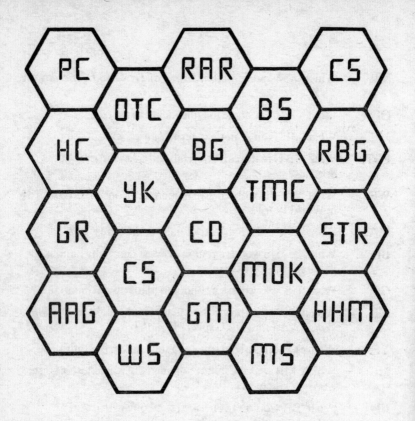

PC	....	CD	....
HC	....	GM	....
GR	....	BS	....
AAG	....	TMC	....
OTC	....	MOK	....
YK	....	MS	....
CS	....	CS	....
WS	....	RBG	....
RAR	....	STR	....
BG	....	HHM	....

PC: What 'PC' is the Welsh name for the Welsh Nationalist Party?

HC: What 'HC' is the law that requires a person to be brought before a court at a stated time?

GR: Which 'GR' was Fred Astaire's partner in such films as *Top Hat*?

AAG: What 'AAG' is an anti-aircraft weapon?

OTC: What 'OTC' means a likely event – particularly if you are playing a game like bridge or rummy?

YK: What 'YK', also known as the Day of Atonement, is the most important Jewish holy day?

CS: What 'CS' is a record of cases at a police station?

WS: What 'WS' is the Roman road that runs from London via St Albans to Wroxeter in Shropshire?

RAR: Which 'RAR' does legend say built the city of Rome?

BG: What 'BG' is the site in East London of the Museum of Childhood?

CD: Which 'CD' composed new music to be played with silent movies such as *Napoleon*?

GM: What 'GM' is a childhood disease, also known as rubella?

BS: What 'BS' measures wind velocity?

TMC: What 'TMC' spoil the broth?

MOK: What 'MOK' was the name of the extremely successful song on a Scottish theme released by Wings in 1977?

MS: What 'MS' is the term applied to a MP's first oration in the House of Commons?

CS: Which 'CS' is Britain's foremost male Marathon runner?

RBG: What 'RBG' at Kew contains rare plants?

STR: What 'STR' means you are liable to spoil the child?

HHM: Which 'HHM' was a writer of macabre stories under the name 'Saki'?

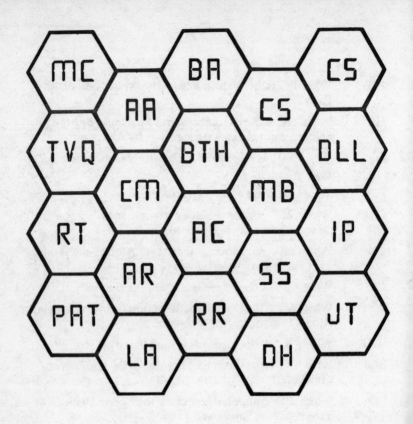

MC	------------------	AC	------------------
TVQ	------------------	RR	------------------
RT	------------------	CS	------------------
PAT	------------------	MB	------------------
AA	------------------	SS	------------------
CM	------------------	DH	------------------
AR	------------------	CS	------------------
LA	------------------	DLL	------------------
BA	------------------	IP	------------------
BTH	------------------	JT	------------------

MC: What 'MC' was a medieval duel to the death?

TVQ: What 'TVQ' was Elizabeth I known as?

RT: What 'RT' is a constantly revised dictionary of English words and phrases?

PAT: What 'PAT' is the play within a play in *A Midsummer Night's Dream*?

AA: What 'AA' is another name for Vitamin C?

CM: What 'CM' is armour composed of rings of metal?

AR: What 'AR' changed into a serpent in the Bible and is the name of a plant?

LA: Which 'LA', known as 'Satchmo', died in 1971?

BA: Which 'BA' was the first man to run on the moon?

BTH: What 'BTH' do you do when patching up an argument – possibly with an axe?

AC: What 'AC' is the name of the submarine telegraph line that links Britain and America?

RR: Which 'RR' is the British architect who designed the Lloyds Building in London and the Hong Kong and Shanghai Bank?

CS: What 'CS' is a swindler at games – particularly poker?

MB: Which 'MB' is an Israeli political leader who won the Nobel Peace Prize in 1978?

SS: What 'SS' do draughtsmen use to draw angles with?

DH: Which 'DH' is the most capped English Rugby Union full-back?

CS: What 'CS' had a number one hit with 'Happy Talk' in 1982?

DLL: What 'DLL' is also known as a crane fly?

IP: What 'IP' is a collective name for Spain and Portugal?

JT: Which 'JT' starred in *Monsieur Hulot's Holiday* and *Traffic*?

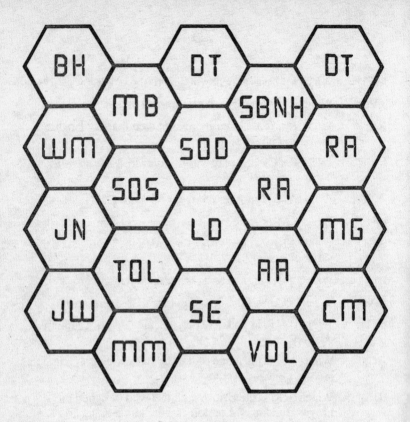

BH	------------------	LD	------------------
WM	------------------	SE	------------------
JN	------------------	SBNH	------------------
JW	------------------	RA	------------------
MB	------------------	AA	------------------
SOS	------------------	VDL	------------------
TOL	------------------	DT	------------------
MM	------------------	RA	------------------
DT	------------------	MG	------------------
SOD	------------------	CM	------------------

BH: What 'BH' is the home of many Hollywood film stars?

WM: What 'WM' is practised by good witches?

JN: Which 'JN' was the first golfer to win the US Masters title two years in succession?

JW: What 'JW' is a pedestrian who walks in the street without paying attention to the traffic?

MB: Which 'MB' were credited with the invention of the hot air balloon?

SOS: What 'SOS' was stolen but now is returned to the throne?

TOL: What 'TOL' must always have ravens living in it if England is not to fall?

MM: What 'MM' involving Myra Hindley was re-opened in 1986?

DT: What 'DT' are hallucinations suffered by an alcoholic?

SOD: What 'SOD' is the symbol of Judaism formed by two interwoven triangles?

LD: What 'LD' is the setting for Arthur Ransome's 'Swallow and Amazon' books?

SE: Which 'SE' sang the theme tune for the James Bond film *For Your Eyes Only*?

SBNH: What 'SBNH' were good Victorian children meant to be?

RA: Which 'RA' directed the films *M*A*S*H* and *Nashville*?

AA: What 'AA' is the thyroid cartilage in the throat?

VDL: What 'VDL' was the original name for Tasmania?

DT: Which 'DT' was the poet whose autobiography is called *Portrait of the Artist as a Young Dog*?

RA: What 'RA' is needed after a bill has passed through Parliament to make it law – it must be obtained from the Queen?

MG: Which 'MG' runs America's most famous ballet company, based in New York?

CM: What 'CM' is played by a small group of orchestral instruments – particularly in a room in a house?

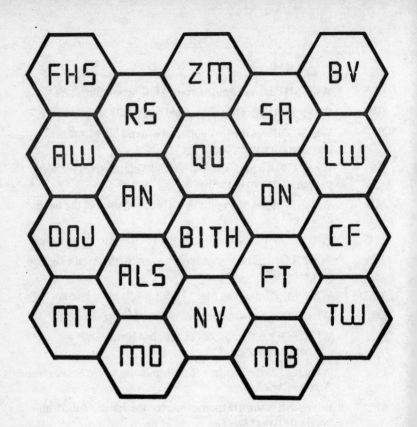

FHS	------------------	BITH	------------------
AW	------------------	NV	------------------
DOJ	------------------	SA	------------------
MT	------------------	DN	------------------
RS	------------------	FT	------------------
AN	------------------	MB	------------------
ALS	------------------	BV	------------------
MO	------------------	LW	------------------
ZM	------------------	CF	------------------
QU	------------------	TW	------------------

FHS: What 'FHS' is, in English, the Olympic motto?

AW: What 'AW', begun in 312 BC, runs from Rome to Brindisi?

DOJ: What 'DOJ' will see everyone on trial at the end of the world?

MT: What 'MT' is one's native language?

RS: What 'RS' acts as a partition between the nave and chancel in a church?

AN: What 'AN' is the name given to the 1001 stories told by Scheherazade?

ALS: What 'ALS' is the Scottish song sung particularly on New Year's Eve?

MO: What 'MO' is a system of buying by post?

ZM: What 'ZM' was the best-selling album of 1980 for the Police?

QU: What 'QU' is an educational institution in Belfast?

BITH: What 'BITH' is worth two in a bush?

NV: What 'NV' was the film starring the young Elizabeth Taylor based on the novel by Enid Bagnold?

SA: Which 'SA' was Nixon's Vice-President and resigned in 1973 during the Watergate affair?

DN: What 'DN' is also known as belladonna?

FT: What 'FT' is a non-active supporter of Communist politics?

MB: What 'MB' is the opera which has Cio-Cio-San as its heroine?

BV: What 'BV' is unrhymed poetry?

LW: What 'LW' do people like to be the one to say at the end of an argument?

CF: What 'CF' causes ox-bow bends in rivers?

TW: What 'TW' is an inlet of the sea that indents the Lincoln/Norfolk coast?

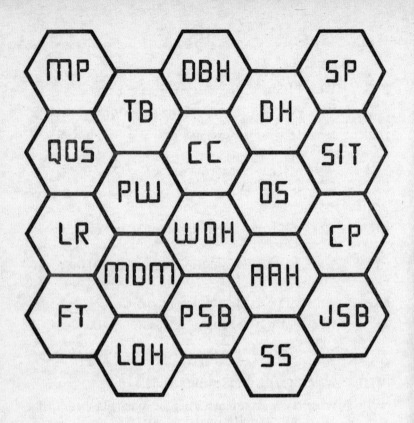

MP	-------------------		WOH	-------------------
QOS	-------------------		PSB	-------------------
LR	-------------------		DH	-------------------
FT	-------------------		OS	-------------------
TB	-------------------		AAH	-------------------
PW	-------------------		SS	-------------------
MDM	-------------------		SP	-------------------
LOH	-------------------		SIT	-------------------
DBH	-------------------		CP	-------------------
CC	-------------------		JSB	-------------------

MP.   What 'MP' was a medieval dramatic representation of the lives of Christ or the Saints?

QOS: What 'QOS' is the card that must be paired with the Jack of Diamonds to make a bezique?

LR: What 'LR' is the capital of the State of Arkansas?

FT: What 'FT' is a form of light fitting filled with argon?

TB: What 'TB's are the sensory organs in the tongue and palate?

PW: Which 'PW' wrote a controversial book about the British Secret service which led to a trial in Australia in 1986?

MDM: What 'MDM' is another term for seasickness?

LOH: What 'LOH' included the cleansing of the Augean Stables?

DBH: What 'DBH's are refuges for destitute children?

CC: What 'CC' was Muhammad Ali's original name?

WOH: What 'WOH' binds a gentleman to a verbal promise?

PSB: Which 'PSB' brought out *Disco*, featuring 'West End Girls' and 'Opportunities', in 1986?

DH: What 'DH' did aristocratic widows move into?

OS: What 'OS' is a famous magic phrase from the Arabian Nights?

AAH: What 'AAH' were a monk and nun who had a tragic love affair in the Middle Ages?

SS: Which 'SS' played the part of the goalkeeper in *Escape to Victory*?

SP: What 'SP' can you try and make out of a sow's ear, but probably unsuccessfully?

SIT: What 'SIT' saves nine?

CP: What 'CP's do the Cellnet division of British Telecom specialise in?

JSB: Which 'JSB' composed the series of piano pieces called *The Well-Tempered Clavier*?

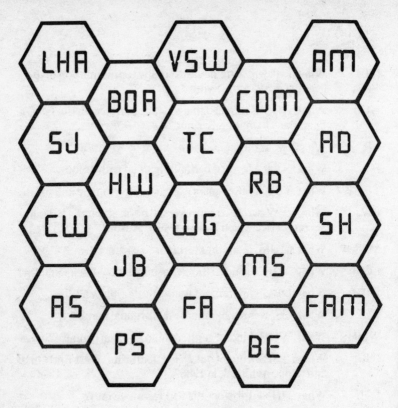

LHA	--------------------	WG	--------------------
SJ	--------------------	FA	--------------------
CW	--------------------	CDM	--------------------
AS	--------------------	RB	--------------------
BOA	--------------------	MS	--------------------
HW	--------------------	BE	--------------------
JB	--------------------	AM	--------------------
PS	--------------------	AD	--------------------
VSW	--------------------	SH	--------------------
TC	--------------------	FAM	--------------------

LHA: What 'LHA' is the top British naval officer?

SJ: Which 'SJ' was a famous ragtime composer – his music was used as the theme for the film *The Sting*?

CW: What 'CW' is a rotating firework?

AS: What 'AS' is the part of the Mediterranean between Italy and Yugoslavia?

BOA: What 'BOA' is Shakespeare known as?

HW: What 'HW' is Cliff Richard's real name?

JB: Which 'JB' was the last British squash player to win the British Open Championship for men?

PS: What 'PS' had the fatted calf for dinner?

VSW: Which 'VSW' owned Sissinghurst and was the model for Virginia Woolf's *Orlando*?

TC: What 'TC', also known as the Decalogue, were brought down from Mount Sinai?

WG: What 'WG' is a scarecrow played by John Pertwee on television?

FA: Which 'FA' is a British dancer who choreographed the film of *The Tales of Beatrix Potter*?

CDM: What 'CDM' is a sweet liqueur made from mint?

RB: Which 'RB' was an English 13th century scientist credited with the discovery of gunpowder?

MS: What 'MS' is dappled with small white fleecy clouds?

BE: What 'BE' is a bird of prey and national emblem of the USA?

AM: What 'AM' indicates that silver is 92.5 per cent pure?

AD: What 'AD' claimed the murder of the head of Renault cars in 1986 in France?

SH: What 'SH' was Napoleon's final place of exile?

FAM: What 'FAM' is a very serious disease of cattle which requires them to be put in strict quarantine?

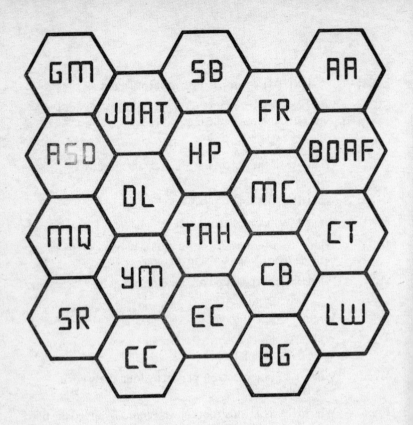

GM	----------------	TAH	----------------
ASD	----------------	EC	----------------
MQ	----------------	FR	----------------
SR	----------------	MC	----------------
JOAT	----------------	CB	----------------
DL	----------------	BG	----------------
YM	----------------	AA	----------------
CC	----------------	BOAF	----------------
SB	----------------	CT	----------------
HP	----------------	LW	----------------

28

GM: Which 'GM' known as 'Suggs' is the vocalist for Madness?

ASD: What 'ASD' is a celebration of holy people on November 1st?

MQ: Which 'MQ', a leading fashion designer, is credited with the invention of the mini skirt?

SR: Which 'SR' had a famous hotel in Singapore named after him?

JOAT: What 'JOAT' is someone who can turn their hand to any kind of work?

DL: What 'DL' is a safe light used in mining?

YM: What 'YM' is written by Jonathan Lynn and Anthony Jay for TV?

CC: What 'CC' is played with a bit of string held between two hands?

SB: Which 'SB' was a very famous French actress at the turn of the century?

HP: What 'HP' do you eat when you are being submissive and admitting you are in the wrong?

TAH: Which 'TAH' are king and queen of Athens in *A Midsummer Night's Dream*?

EC: What 'EC' is the name of the diplomatic agreement between Britain and France?

FR: What 'FR' is a yachting competition held between Cowes and Plymouth?

MC: What 'MC' uses dots and dashes?

CB: Which 'CB' invented a mathematical calculating machine that was the forerunner of the computer?

BG: What 'BG' was an American movement of the 1950s which included Jack Kerouac and Alan Ginsberg?

AA: What 'AA' is the capital of Ethiopia?

BOAF: What 'BOAF' flock together?

CT: What 'CT's do you have four of between your incisors and molars?

LW: Which 'LW' is leader of Solidarity?

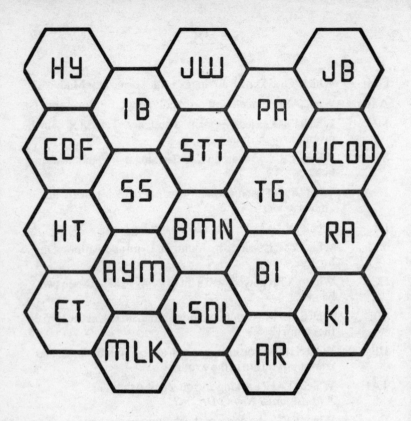

HY	-----------------	BMN	-----------------
CDF	-----------------	LSDL	-----------------
HT	-----------------	PA	-----------------
CT	-----------------	TG	-----------------
IB	-----------------	BI	-----------------
SS	-----------------	AR	-----------------
AYM	-----------------	JB	-----------------
MLK	-----------------	WCOD	-----------------
JW	-----------------	RA	-----------------
STT	-----------------	KI	-----------------

29

HY: What 'HY' War was the Battle of Agincourt fought in?

CDF: What 'CDF' is a form of baccarat?

HT: What 'HT' buildings have black and white fronts?

CT: Which 'CT' had albums called *Victorialand* and *Head Over Heels*?

IB: Which 'IB' decided in 1986 to spend 6 months in England and 6 months in Australia?

SS: What 'SS' is a boat built on the same lines as another one?

AYM: What 'AYM' included John Osborne, Kingsley Amis and John Braine in the 1950s?

MLK: Which 'MLK' now has a national holiday in his honour in the USA?

JW: Which 'JW' played Tarzan and won five Olympic swimming medals?

STT: What 'STT' is an extinct member of the cat family with tusk-like teeth?

BMN: What 'BMN' is a card game you might play with the person next-door?

LSDL: What 'LSDL' is a recommendation not to disturb lazy canines, but to leave things as they are?

PA: Which 'PA' was the Greek goddess of wisdom?

TG: What 'TG' is a bromide compound used in riots to cause a temporary loss of sight?

BI: What 'BI' is the piece of land which lies between Greenland and Canada?

AR: What 'AR' is mouth to mouth resuscitation a form of?

JB: What 'JB' is a way of describing a poorly and hastily constructed house?

WCOD: What 'WCOD' did Vera Lynn tell us there would be bluebirds over?

RA: What 'RA' is a legislation used to disperse an unlawful or unruly assembly of people?

KI: What 'KI' is the site of several bombings of tankers in the Iranian Gulf?

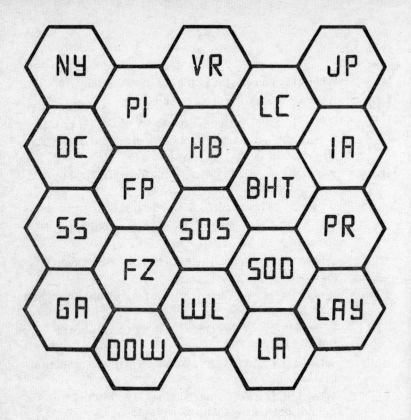

NT	------------------	SOS	------------------
DC	------------------	WL	------------------
SS	------------------	LC	------------------
GA	------------------	BHT	------------------
PI	------------------	SOD	------------------
FP	------------------	LA	------------------
FZ	------------------	JP	------------------
DOW	------------------	IA	------------------
VR	------------------	PR	------------------
HB	------------------	LAY	------------------

30

NT: Which 'NT' accused the BBC of left-wing bias in 1986?

DC: What 'DC' is a form of bravery found with the aid of drink – possibly in Holland?

SS: What 'SS' include baptism, confirmation, matrimony and extreme unction?

GA: Which 'GA' designed and directed *Thunderbirds*?

PI: What 'PI' include drums, triangles and cymbals?

FP: What 'FP' is 32° Farenheit?

FZ: Which 'FZ' has produced and directed films of the operas *Otello* and *Don Giovanni*?

DOW: Which 'DOW' appears on five pound notes?

VR: Which 'VR' was Hitler's foreign minister from 1938–1945?

HB: What 'HB' do you use to steer a bicycle?

SOS: What 'SOS' had a hit with 'Breakout' in 1986?

WL: What 'WL' is a sleeping car on a continental railway?

LC: What 'LC' is a collective name for the Netherlands, Belgium and Luxembourg?

BHT: What 'BHT' are a major riding event that takes place at the home of the Duke of Beaufort in Gloucestershire?

SOD: What 'SOD' is said to hang over the head of someone in danger – it originally hung by a hair over an Ancient Greek?

LA: What 'LA' uses drugs to produce a loss of sensation in only one part of the body?

JP: What 'JP' is the highest win on a fruit-machine?

IA: Which 'IA' is the American science-fiction writer with his own Sci-Fi magazine?

PR: What 'PR' is a reform in the electoral system which the Liberal Party strongly support?

LAY: What 'LAY' were the opposing houses in the War of the Roses?

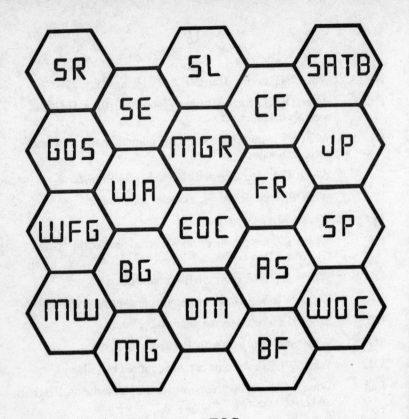

SR	------------------	EOC	------------------
GOS	------------------	DM	------------------
WFG	------------------	CF	------------------
MW	------------------	FR	------------------
SE	------------------	AS	------------------
WA	------------------	BF	------------------
BG	------------------	SATB	------------------
MG	------------------	JP	------------------
SL	------------------	SP	------------------
MGR	------------------	WOE	------------------

SR: What 'SR' is 9 of 81?

GOS: What 'GOS' is the address of the Children's Hospital in London?

WFG: What 'WFG' is Samuel Beckett's most famous play?

MW: What 'MW' is also known as the Via Lactea?

SE: What 'SE' does someone who excels set that we should all follow – like a star?

WA: What 'WA' was the name given to counter-revolutionary forces in Bolshevik Russia?

BG: What 'BG' had 'tell Sid' as its advertising slogan in 1986?

MG: Which 'MG' is the most capped Irish Rugby player?

SL: What 'SL' is the river Quebec City is built on?

MGR: What 'MGR' is a carousel?

EOC: What 'EOC' is the body that ensures there is no racial or sexual discrimination, particularly in jobs?

DM: Which 'DM' commanded the US forces in Southeast Asia in World War II?

CF: What 'CF' is a very small amount – maybe given to poultry to eat?

FR: What 'FR' is a children's TV programme devised by the Muppet master Jim Henson?

AS: What 'AS' is also known as the Yeti?

BF: What 'BF' is a matador?

SATB: Which 'SATB' has hits with 'Israel' and 'Happy House'?

JP: Which 'JP' presents a request show on Radio 1 on Sunday evenings?

SP: Which 'SP' is famous for his diaries written in the 17th century?

WOE: What 'WOE' is the albumen?

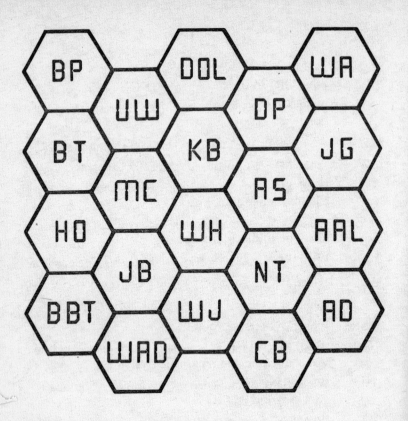

BP	------------------	WH	------------------
BT	------------------	WJ	------------------
HO	------------------	DP	------------------
BBT	------------------	AS	------------------
UW	------------------	NT	------------------
MC	------------------	CB	------------------
JB	------------------	WA	------------------
WAD	------------------	JG	------------------
DOL	------------------	AAL	------------------
KB	------------------	AD	------------------

32

BP: What 'BP' is a result of septicaemia?

BT: Which 'BT' is David Copperfield's aunt?

HO: What 'HO' are macassar and Bay Rum types of?

BBT: What 'BBT' says that the universe started with an immense explosion?

UW: What 'UW's have no names and are buried at Westminster Abbey, the Arc de Triomphe and other places?

MC: Which 'MC' starred in *Barnum* and *Phantom of the Opera*?

JB: What 'JB' might you call someone who has been to prison, or in a cage?

WAD: What 'WAD' was walls made of sticks and clay?

DOL: What 'DOL' was Norman Tebbit made Chancellor of in 1985?

KB: What 'KB' do soldiers carry their belongings in – and maybe their troubles?

WH: What 'WH' was Kate Bush's first single and a number one hit in 1978?

WJ: Which 'WJ' is a man destined to roam the earth forever?

DP: Which 'DP' wrote *Pennies From Heaven* and *The Singing Detective*?

AS: What 'AS' were the English people before the Norman conquest?

NT: What 'NT' tried Nazi leaders for war crimes?

CB: Which 'CB' is a famous British photographer who designed the film version of *My Fair Lady*?

WA: In what 'WA' are the monarchs of Great Britain crowned?

JG: Which 'JG' was the West Indian cricketer awarded an MBE in 1985?

AAL: What 'AAL' is the distance you might keep something you don't trust?

AD: What 'AD' is an island sheikdom of the United Arab Emirates?

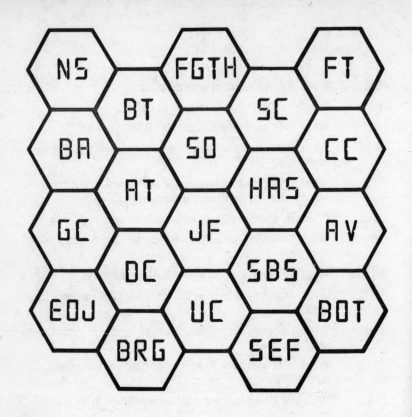

NS	-------------------	JF	-------------------
BA	-------------------	UC	-------------------
GC	-------------------	SC	-------------------
EOJ	-------------------	HAS	-------------------
BT	-------------------	SBS	-------------------
AT	-------------------	SEF	-------------------
DC	-------------------	FT	-------------------
BRG	-------------------	CC	-------------------
FGTH	-------------------	AV	-------------------
SO	-------------------	BOT	-------------------

33

NS: What 'NS' is the name for Darwin's theory of the survival of the fittest in nature?

BA: What 'BA' is the name given to the period when man first used metal for tools?

GC: What 'GC' is an uninvited intruder at a party?

EOJ: What 'EOJ' was a Mikado?

BT: What 'BT' commemorates the conquest of England by William the Conqueror?

AT: Which 'AT' was the black South African churchman who won the Nobel Peace Prize in 1985?

DC: What 'DC' was Africa sometimes known as?

BRG: What 'BRG' is a timetable of all passenger trains running in Great Britain?

FGTH: What 'FGTH' recorded 'War' and 'Relax'?

SO: What 'SO' is a bitter fruit used to make marmalade?

JF: Which 'JF' became World Heavyweight Boxing Champion in 1968 after Muhammad Ali was stripped of the title?

UC: What 'UC' is the term used for capital letters in printing?

SC: Which 'SC' starred in the film *The Name of the Rose*?

HAS: What 'HAS' symbolise the worker and the peasant on the Russian flag?

SBS: What 'SBS' is the arts programme Melvyn Bragg presents?

SEF: What 'SEF' is caused by static electricity and sometimes seen striking the masts of ships?

FT: Which 'FT's use tarot cards?

CC: What 'CC' disappeared leaving only its grin behind?

AV: What 'AV' is the English translation of the Bible published in 1611?

BOT: What 'BOT' is the British town that was neutral territory between Scotland and England for 300 years?

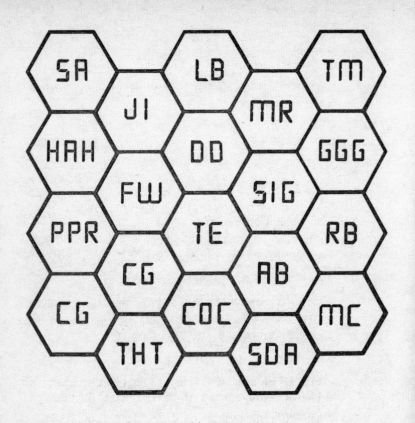

SA	------------------	TE	------------------
HAH	------------------	COC	------------------
PPR	------------------	MR	------------------
CG	------------------	SIG	------------------
JI	------------------	AB	------------------
FW	------------------	SDA	------------------
CG	------------------	TM	------------------
THT	------------------	GGG	------------------
LB	------------------	RB	------------------
DD	------------------	MC	------------------

34

SA: What 'SA' arrived when Sir Francis Drake was playing bowls?

HAH: What 'HAH' is a paper-chase?

PPR: Which 'PPR' was a 16th-century Flemish painter who was also a diplomat in London?

CG: What 'CG' is an American convict part of while doing hard labour?

JI: Which 'JI' starred in *The Mission* and *Brideshead Revisited*?

FW: What 'FW' do you bear if you are lying, particularly in court?

CG: Which 'CG' has been political leader of Libya since 1969?

THT: 'THT' are which star sign, also known as Gemini?

LB: Which 'LB' invented moving pictures in 1895?

DD: What 'DD' will do very reckless things without thinking first?

TE: What 'TE' happens when the moon passes exactly in front of the sun?

COC: What 'COC' elects the Pope?

MR: What 'MR' is carved with the heads of four American Presidents?

SIG: What 'SIG' is a phrase someone uses when they are welcoming quietness – perhaps of a particularly rich kind?

AB: Which 'AB' wrote *Anna of the Five Towns*?

SDA: What 'SDA' are a Christian sect who observe Saturday as the Sabbath?

TM: Which 'TM' is an ITV newspresenter and wrote the biography of cricketer Clive Lloyd?

GGG: What 'GGG' is the phrase an auctioneer completes a sale with?

RB: Which 'RB' was the nickname of a World War I German air ace – a great enemy of Snoopy's?

MC: What 'MC' is an inflammatory hand-grenade named after a Soviet Commissar, who died in 1986?

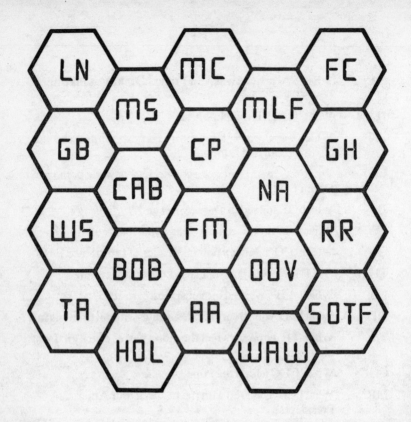

LN	\-\-\-\-\-\-\-\-\-\-\-\-\-\-\-\-\-\-	FM	\-\-\-\-\-\-\-\-\-\-\-\-\-\-\-\-\-\-
GB	------------------	AA	------------------
WS	------------------	MLF	------------------
TA	------------------	NA	------------------
MS	------------------	OOV	------------------
CAB	------------------	WAW	------------------
BOB	------------------	FC	------------------
HOL	------------------	GH	------------------
MC	------------------	RR	------------------
CP	------------------	SOTF	------------------

35

LN: What 'LN' in Scotland is the home of a monster?

GB: What 'GB' covers the door that separates servants from the main house, and also snooker tables?

WS: Which 'WS' became the Duchess of Windsor?

TA: What 'TA' is the cricket trophy given to the winner of the Test Series between England and Australia?

MS: What 'MS' is the planet Venus also known as?

CAB: What 'CAB' are the jester's badge of office?

BOB: What 'BOB' was the scene of Richard III's defeat by Henry VII?

HOL: What 'HOL' is the highest court of appeal in Britain?

MC: What 'MC' suffered a disastrous earthquake in 1985, but went on to host a major sporting event in 1986?

CP: What 'CP' is an easy task – even infants can do it?

FM: Which 'FM' helped Bonnie Prince Charlie escape from Scotland?

AA: What 'AA' is the official name for an Oscar?

MLF: Which 'MLF' bewitched Merlin and was King Arthur's half-sister?

NA: Which 'NA' was the first woman to sit in the House of Commons?

OOV: What 'OOV' is concentrated sulphuric acid?

WAW: What 'WAW' are the threads stretched on a loom?

FC: What 'FC' are kings, queens and jacks known as in a playing pack?

GH: Which 'GH' presents *Sunday Sunday* on television?

RR: Which 'RR' is the Archbishop of Canterbury?

SOTF: What 'SOTF' does someone do who is remaining neutral – possibly between two fields?

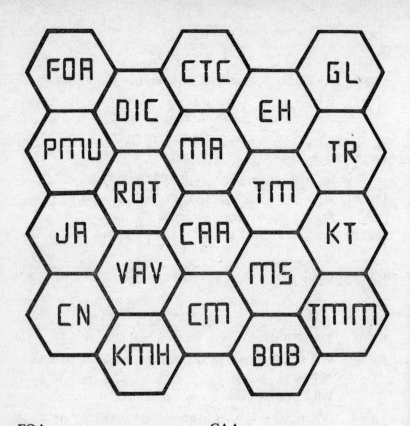

FOA	-----------------	CAA	-----------------
PMU	-----------------	CM	-----------------
JA	-----------------	EH	-----------------
CN	-----------------	TM	-----------------
DIC	-----------------	MS	-----------------
ROT	-----------------	BOB	-----------------
VAV	-----------------	GL	-----------------
KMH	-----------------	TR	-----------------
CTC	-----------------	KT	-----------------
MA	-----------------	TMM	-----------------

36

FOA: What 'FOA' in Warwickshire is the setting for *As You Like It?*

PMU: What 'PMU' is a stimulating drink after a previous depression or over-indulgence?

JA: Which 'JA' resigned his position as deputy Chairman of the Conservative Party in 1986?

CN: What 'CN' is another name for the Mafia?

DIC: What 'DIC' were the architectural orders of Greek temples, and particularly their columns?

ROT: What 'ROT', during which 2500 people were executed, was the final period of the French Revolution?

VAV: What 'VAV' is a small raised pie, often containing chicken?

KMH: What 'KMH' are reported to be Nelson's last words?

CTC: What 'CTC' does a cow do when eating?

MA: Which 'MA' presents the television quiz programme *Child's Play?*

CAA: Which 'CAA' were the sons of Adam and Eve?

CM: What 'CM' is a poisonous, colourless gas occurring in exhaust fumes?

EH: What 'EH' is an intellectual sometimes known as – particularly if he has a domed forehead?

TM: What 'TM' was built by Shah Jehan in India as a tomb for his wife?

MS: What 'MS' lies between Chile and Tierra del Fuego and connects the Atlantic and Pacific Oceans?

BOB: What 'BOB' is a double sirloin of meat?

GL: Which 'GL' scored most goals for England in the 1986 World Cup?

TR: What 'TR' were the names of regions in Yorkshire which were abolished in 1974?

KT: What 'KT' wore a white tunic with a red cross and were a brotherhood originally formed to protect pilgrims to Jerusalem?

TMM: What 'TMM' is a nickname for that jolly King Charles II?

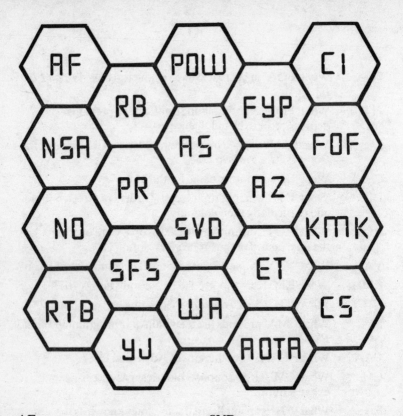

AF	------------------	SVD	------------------
NSA	------------------	WA	------------------
NO	------------------	FYP	------------------
RTB	------------------	AZ	------------------
RB	------------------	ET	------------------
PR	------------------	AOTA	------------------
SFS	------------------	CI	------------------
YJ	------------------	FOF	------------------
POW	------------------	KMK	------------------
AS	------------------	CS	------------------

37

AF: What 'AF' is caused by microscopic fungi between the toes?

NSA: What 'NSA' is another name for Neolithic?

NO: What 'NO' do people look after if they are being selfish?

RTB: Which 'RTB' was inspired to fight again by a spider?

RB: What 'RB' is a famous patriotic composition of Thomas Arne's?

PR: Which 'PR' married Grace Kelly in 1956?

SFS: What 'SFS' make up the pattern on a chess board?

YJ: What 'YJ' is awarded to the leader of the racers each day in the Tour de France?

POW: What 'POW' was a title created by Edward I for his eldest son?

AS: Which 'AS' is President of the National Union of Miners?

SVD: What 'SVD' is an illness characterised by jerky convulsive movements?

WA: Which 'WA' directed *Manhattan* and *Hannah and Her Sisters*?

FYP: What 'FYP' is a limited period time on which is based the Russian Economy?

AZ: What 'AZ', at minus 273.15° Centigrade, is the lowest possible temperature?

ET: What 'ET' is French for a naughty child?

AOTA: What 'AOTA' is the fifth book of the New Testament?

CI: Which 'CI' is the English novelist who wrote *Goodbye to Berlin* on which the film *Cabaret* was based?

FOF: What 'FOF' is someone who is laughed at and held up to ridicule?

KMK: What 'KMK' is a musical based on *The Taming of the Shrew*?

CS: What 'CS' do Hindus believe in and is comprised of Brahmins, Kshatriyas, Vaisyas and Sudras?

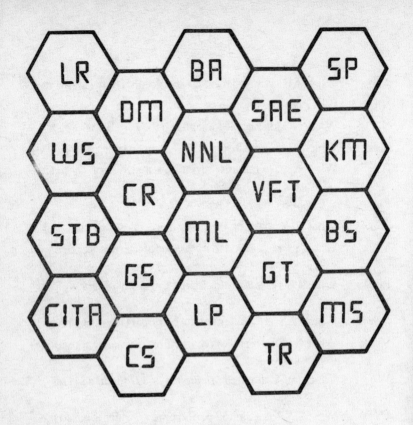

LR	------------------	ML	------------------
WS	------------------	LP	------------------
STB	------------------	SAE	------------------
CITA	------------------	VFT	------------------
DM	------------------	GT	------------------
CR	------------------	TR	------------------
GS	------------------	SP	------------------
CS	------------------	KM	------------------
BA	------------------	BS	------------------
NNL	------------------	MS	------------------

38

LR: Which 'LR' was the first director-general of the BBC?

WS: What 'WS' is America's financial centre?

STB: Which 'STB' is Olivia's cousin in *Twelfth Night*?

CITA: What 'CITA' might you build if you were day-dreaming?

DM: What 'DM' was the newspaper responsible for bringing Zola Budd to Britain?

CR: What 'CR' is the basis of the Greek dish taramasalata?

GS: What 'GS' is another name for an alsatian dog?

CS: What 'CS' is a narrow miss – particularly with a razor?

BA: What 'BA' was the site of several US atomic bomb tests?

NNL: What 'NNL' is the home of Peter Pan?

ML: Which 'ML' started the Protestant Reformation in Germany?

LP: What 'LP' do you use in an acid test?

SAE: What 'SAE' is the command given to soldiers when they can relax slightly?

VFT: What 'VFT' is a plant that feeds on insects?

GT: What 'GT' describes someone who has travelled all over the world?

TR: What 'TR' was the name Hitler gave to his dictatorship?

SP: On what 'SP' is Stonehenge sited?

KM: Which 'KM' in Greek mythology ruled Crete and was master of the minotaur?

BS: What 'BS' is the terrorist movement ETA associated with?

MS: Which 'MS' starred in *The French Lieutenant's Woman* and *Out of Africa*?

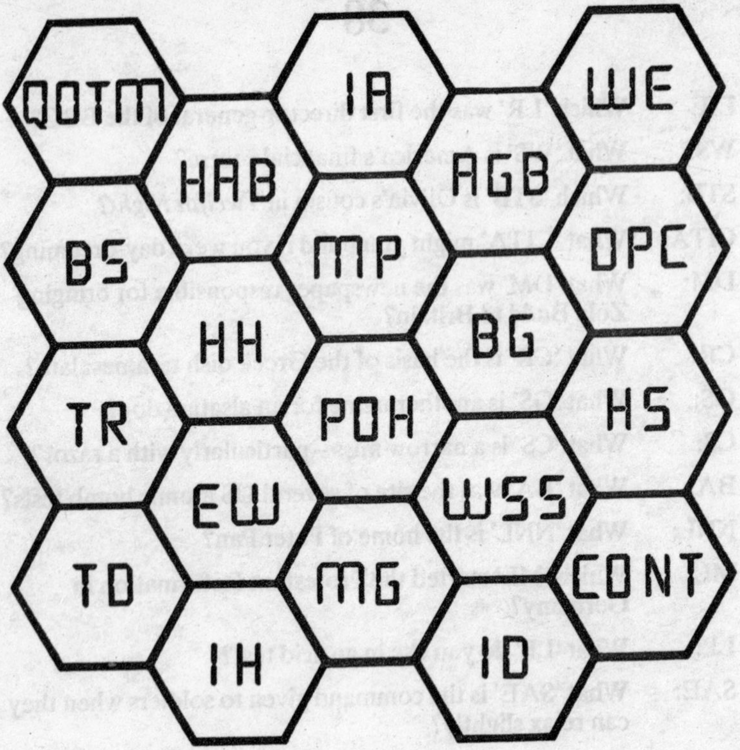

QOTM
IA
WE
HAB
AGB
BS
MP
DPC
HH
BG
TR
POH
HS
EW
WSS
TD
MG
CONT
IH
ID

QOTM -------------------

BS -------------------

TR -------------------

TD -------------------

HAB -------------------

HH -------------------

EW -------------------

IH -------------------

IA -------------------

MP -------------------

POH -------------------

MG -------------------

AGB -------------------

BG -------------------

WSS -------------------

ID -------------------

WE -------------------

DPC -------------------

HS -------------------

CONT -------------------

39

QOTM: What 'QOTM' might a pretty girl be chosen to be in early Summer?

BS: What 'BS' is a mathematical system that uses 2 instead of 10 as its base?

TR: What 'TR' stars Corbett and Barker?

TD: What 'TD' is a gesture made with the hand meaning a refusal?

HAB: Which 'HAB' are two comic and musical ladies (or possibly not)?

HH: What 'HH' forms a boundary to a park in a sunken ditch?

EW: Which 'EW' made famous the phrase 'up and under'?

IH: What 'IH' is the strong force that lies in a velvet glove?

IA: Which 'IA' was deposed in Uganda in 1979?

MP: Which 'MP' was nanny in Cherry Tree Lane?

POH: What 'POH' are rocks on either side of the Strait of Gibraltar?

MG: What 'MG' is a balcony for musicians which you might find in a medieval hall?

AGB: Which 'AGB' invented the telephone?

BG: What 'BG's are A, AB, B and O?

WSS: What 'WSS' is a musical based on *Romeo and Juliet*?

ID: What 'ID' is a Latin phrase meaning beneath one's dignity?

WE: What 'WE' might someone have if they have a squint?

DPC: What 'DPC' keeps the wet out of walls?

HS: What 'HS' was the site of a horrific football riot that led to Liverpool F.C. being banned from Europe?

CONT: What 'CONT' is a rope whip formerly used for flogging sailors?

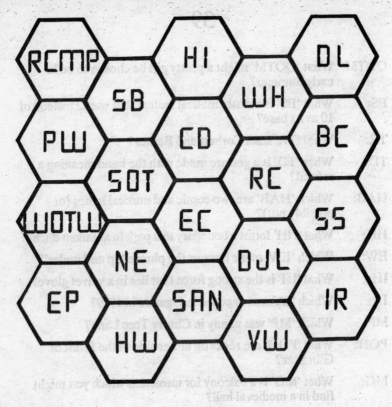

Abbr.	Answer line	Abbr.	Answer line
RCMP	-----------------	EC	-----------------
PW	-----------------	SAN	-----------------
WOTW	-----------------	WH	-----------------
EP	-----------------	RC	-----------------
SB	-----------------	DJL	-----------------
SOT	-----------------	VW	-----------------
NE	-----------------	DL	-----------------
HW	-----------------	BC	-----------------
HI	-----------------	SS	-----------------
CD	-----------------	IR	-----------------

40

RCMP: Which 'RCMP' always get their man?

PW: Which 'PW' pretended to be Richard, son of Edward IV?

WOTW: What 'WOTW' is fen-fire known as because it looks like an ethereal being?

EP: What 'EP' include electrons, protons, neutrons and neutrinos?

SB: Which 'SB' is the patron of mountaineers and had a large dog named after him?

SOT: What 'SOT' is the main event in Homer's *Iliad*?

NE: What 'NE' was the old collective name for Turkey and the Balkan States?

HW: What 'HW' ran from Wallsend-on-Tyne to Bowness?

HI: What 'HI' were massacred by Herod and have a feast day on 28 December?

CD: What 'CD' is the American President's country retreat, famous for an Israeli-Arab meeting?

EC: What 'EC' is a vehicle with an extra large boot?

SAN: What 'SAN' was the film made in 1986 about the Sex Pistols?

WH: What 'WH' is a wild African pig with tusks and an ugly face?

RC: What 'RC' dating method is used by archaeologists to measure the age of objects?

DJL: What 'DJL' do sailors call a watery grave?

VW: Which 'VW' was the first woman to be elected to the All England Lawn Tennis committee?

DL: Which 'DL' is a religious leader, believed to be a reincarnation of his predecessors?

BC: What 'BC' used to be the name of Zaire?

SS: What 'SS' is another name for an agony aunt?

IR: What 'IR' collects income tax in Britain?

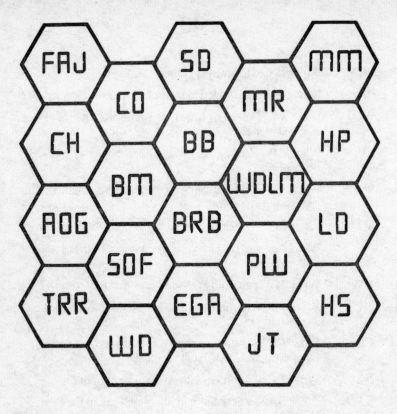

FAJ	------------------	BRB	------------------
CH	------------------	EGA	------------------
AOG	------------------	MR	------------------
TRR	------------------	WDLM	------------------
CO	------------------	PW	------------------
BM	------------------	JT	------------------
SOF	------------------	MM	------------------
WD	------------------	HP	------------------
SD	------------------	LD	------------------
BB	------------------	HS	------------------

41

FAJ: What 'FAJ' are goods lost at sea known as?

CH: What 'CH' are a limestone range found mainly in Gloucestershire?

AOG: What 'AOG' is the operation of uncontrollable forces of nature?

TRR: Which 'TRR' recorded 'Bang Zoom Let's Go-Go!' in 1986?

CO: What 'CO's are people who feel it morally wrong to fight in wars?

BM: What 'BM' is an infamous German terrorist group?

SOF: What 'SOF' is another term for a mercenary – possibly a warrior looking for luck?

WD: What 'WD' is a small, extremely dense star with a low luminosity?

SD: What 'SD' was the name of the first English passenger railway line?

BB: Which 'BB' is the tennis player with a 150 mph service?

BRB: What 'BRB' are men engaged in secret research?

EGA: Which 'EGA' was the founder of a Hospital for Women in London?

MR: What 'MR' is the sporting event named after a 150 mile run by Pheidippides in Ancient Greece?

WDLM: Which 'WDLM' wrote the poem beginning '"Is there anybody there?" said the Traveller.'?

PW: What 'PW' was the man who used to operate a primitive air-conditioning system in India?

JT: Which 'JT' retired from presenting *Today* on Radio 4 at the end of 1986?

MM: What 'MM' are a particular kind of English folk-dancers?

HP: Which 'HP' wrote *The Caretaker* and *The Birthday Party*?

LD: What 'LD' do people take pity on – particularly if it's a crippled bird?

HS: What 'HS' starring Bing Crosby and Grace Kelly is the musical version of *Philadelphia Story*?

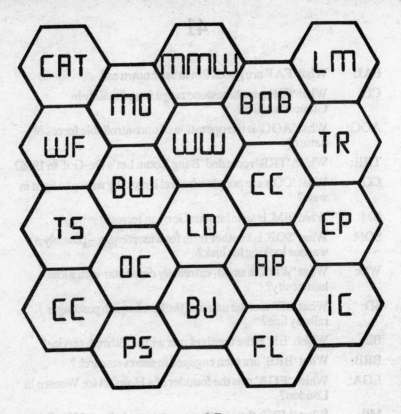

CAT	--------------------	LD	--------------------
WF	--------------------	BJ	--------------------
TS	--------------------	BOB	--------------------
CC	--------------------	CC	--------------------
MO	--------------------	AP	--------------------
BW	--------------------	FL	--------------------
OC	--------------------	LM	--------------------
PS	--------------------	TR	--------------------
MMW	--------------------	EP	--------------------
WW	--------------------	IC	--------------------

42

CAT: What 'CAT' are the basic metals that make bronze?

WF: What 'WF' means salaries will not be raised?

TS: Which 'TS' is the titular hero of Laurence Sterne's most famous novel?

CC: Which 'CC' stabbed Marat in his bath during the French Revolution?

MO: What 'MO' do troops, or anyone, receive when commanded to depart?

BW: Which 'BW' starred in *Last of the Summer Wine* and *Porridge*?

OC: What 'OC' does a man who loves his mother too much have?

PS: Which 'PS' was the England goalkeeper in the 1986 World Cup?

MMW: What 'MMW' do you tell someone to do when you want them to pay close attention to what you are saying?

WW: What 'WW' is built on the site of Solomon's temple in Jerusalem?

LD: What 'LD' is also known as a retriever?

BJ: Which 'BJ' recorded 'Uptown Girl' and 'An Innocent Man'?

BOB: What 'BOB' was won by 'the few'?

CC: Which 'CC' starred in *The Kid* and *The Great Dictator*?

AP: What 'AP' is measured by a barometer?

FL: Which 'FL' had an airline called the Skytrain?

LM: What 'LM' is a charming male who is fond of female society?

TR: Which 'TR' by Sheridan features Lydia Languish and Mrs Malaprop?

EP: Which 'EP' was the French singer famous for her passionate songs such as 'Je ne regrette rien?'

IC: What 'IC' is maize?

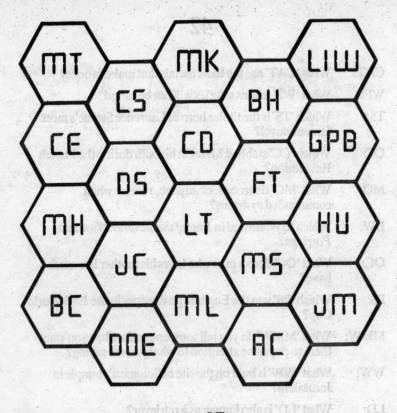

MT	-------------------	LT	-------------------
CE	-------------------	ML	-------------------
MH	-------------------	BH	-------------------
BC	-------------------	FT	-------------------
CS	-------------------	MS	-------------------
DS	-------------------	AC	-------------------
JC	-------------------	LIW	-------------------
DOE	-------------------	GPB	-------------------
MK	-------------------	HU	-------------------
CD	-------------------	JM	-------------------

43

MT: Which 'MT' is the heroine of George Eliot's *Mill on the Floss*?

CE: What 'CE' is the system of state-financed schools in Britain?

MH: What 'MH' is another name for vaudeville?

BC: What 'BC' is another term for contraception?

CS: What 'CS' would it be very unwise to let a bull loose in?

DS: Which 'DS', now with Eurythmics, is an ex-member of The Tourists?

JC: Which 'JC' is the famous French underwater explorer?

DOE: Which 'DOE' is President of the World Wildlife Fund?

MK: What 'MK' is another term for euthanasia?

CD: What 'CD' is the name of a theory to do with movements of large masses of land?

LT: What 'LT's are hazel catkins?

ML: What 'ML' was the fortified Franco-German frontier before World War II?

BH: What 'BH' is another name for a hotel pageboy?

FT: Which 'FT' starred John Cleese and Prunella Scales?

MS: What 'MS' does a good restaurant want to be awarded?

AC: Which 'AC' wrote London's longest running play?

LIW: What 'LIW' is a woman attending on the sovereign?

GPB: What 'GPB' was the book by Anita Loos which was made into a film starring Marilyn Monroe and Jane Russell?

HU: What 'HU' is the educational institution at Cambridge, Massachusetts?

JM: Which 'JM' was asked to resign from Queen's Lawn Tennis Club in 1985?

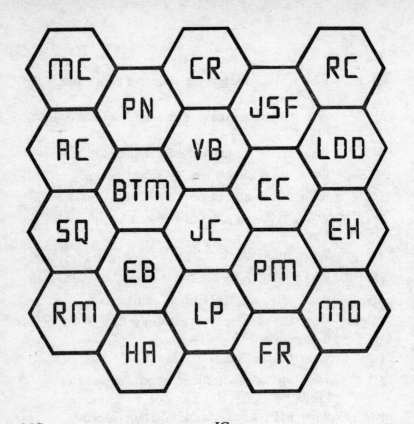

MC	-------------------	JC	-------------------
AC	-------------------	LP	-------------------
SQ	-------------------	JSF	-------------------
RM	-------------------	CC	-------------------
PN	-------------------	PM	-------------------
BTM	-------------------	FR	-------------------
EB	-------------------	RC	-------------------
HA	-------------------	LDD	-------------------
CR	-------------------	EH	-------------------
VB	-------------------	MO	-------------------

44

MC: What 'MC' was obtained from King John in 1215?

AC: What 'AC' marks off the days to Christmas?

SQ: Which 'SQ' recorded 'In the Army Now'?

RM: Which 'RM' is the only unconquered heavyweight boxing champion in the world?

PN: What 'PN' disappeared from English currency in 1986?

BTM: What 'BTM' is the forward part of a ship where common sailors sleep?

EB: Which 'EB' is the heroine of Jane Austen's *Pride and Prejudice*?

HA: What 'HA' are used to help alleviate deafness?

CR: What 'CR' is a chain of rocks made of skeletal material found in warm, shallow seas?

VB: What 'VB' is made of slats and covers a window?

JC: Which 'JC' claimed Australia for Britain in 1770?

LP: What 'LP' is the residence of the Archbishop of Canterbury?

JSF: What 'JSF' was the international version of the game *It's A Knockout*?

CC: What 'CC' is a flimsy material also known as butter muslin?

PM: What 'PM' starred Ryan O'Neill and his daughter Tatum?

FR: What 'FR' in World War II were also known as the Maquis?

RC: What 'RC' by Wagner is performed every year at Bayreuth?

LDD: What 'LDD' is meant to be the way someone speaks or acts when trying to be posh?

EH: Which 'EH' is now a football commentator who was once captain of Liverpool and England?

MO: What 'MO' is also known as a harmonica?

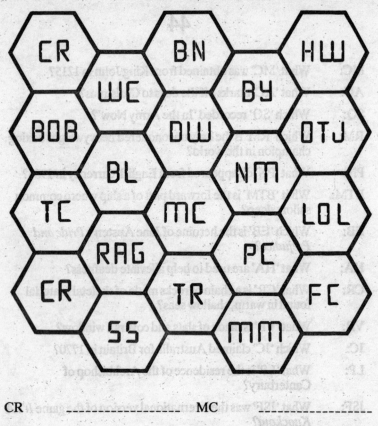

CR		MC	
BOB	-------------------	TR	
TC	-------------------	BY	-------------------
CR		NM	
WC	-------------------	PC	
BL	-------------------	MM	-------------------
RAG		HW	
SS	-------------------	OTJ	-------------------
BN	-------------------	LOL	-------------------
DW	-------------------	FC	-------------------

45

CR: What 'CR' are high energy radiation reaching Earth from outer space?

BOB: What 'BOB' is an animal carrying a heavy load?

TC: Which 'TC' conducted tours round Europe in the 19th century and founded a travel agency?

CR: What 'CR' was a period of ferment in China from 1966–1969?

WC: Which 'WC' lived at Chartwell?

BL: What 'BL' does someone make if going straight for an object – possibly to collect some honey?

RAG: Which 'RAG' are Hamlet's fellow students?

SS: What 'SS' is the longest day of the year?

BN: Which 'BN' presents a film review programme for BBC television?

DW: What 'DW' is a beetle that makes a knocking noise when attacking wood?

MC: What 'MC' does someone who's looking after their own interests have an eye to?

TR: Which 'TR' recorded the 1970s hit 'Glad to Be Gay'?

BY: What 'BY' is an organism used in beer-making from which Marmite is made?

NM: Which 'NM' was the Briton who nearly won the Grand Prix in 1986?

PC: What 'PC' is used for igniting the explosive in cartridges – used on its own it just makes a bang?

MM: Which 'MM' is the part played by Mel Gibson?

HW: What 'HW' will make it difficult to work up a lather with soap?

OTJ: What 'OTJ' is the choral finale of Beethoven's Ninth Symphony?

LOL: What 'LOL' is a task one delights in doing?

FC: Which 'FC' is premier of Cuba?

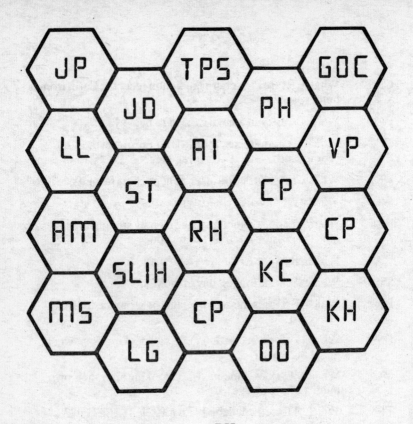

JP	----------------	RH	----------------
LL	----------------	CP	----------------
AM	----------------	PH	----------------
MS	----------------	CP	----------------
JD	----------------	KC	----------------
ST	----------------	DO	----------------
SLIH	----------------	GOC	----------------
LG	----------------	VP	----------------
TPS	----------------	CP	----------------
AI	----------------	KH	----------------

46

JP: Which 'JP' was the first lady trainer to have a horse win the Cheltenham Gold Cup?

LL: What 'LL' describes a country without any sea coast?

AM: Which 'AM' was Director General of the BBC?

MS: What 'MS' do most young European men, and all Israelis, have to do, but was abolished in the UK in 1962?

JD: Which 'JD' recorded the hit 'Free Nelson Mandela' in 1984?

ST: What 'ST's appear on the screen in a foreign language film?

SLIH: What 'SLIH' was the film starring Tony Curtis and Jack Lemmon in drag?

LG: What 'LG' was Capability Brown's profession?

TPS: What 'TPS' is a piece by Holst featuring Saturn and Jupiter?

AI: What 'AI' is Latin for without limit — going on forever?

RH: Which 'RH' is the Australian artist who presents *Cartoon Time*?

CP: What 'CP' was built to house the Great Exhibition in 1851?

PH: What 'PH' is Henry V known as in Shakespeare's *Henry IV* parts One and Two?

CP What 'CP' is an inmate of a particular Royal Hospital for old soldiers?

KC: Which 'KC' tried to command the waves but failed?

DO: What 'DO' did Ancient Greeks consult to find out about the future?

GOC: What 'GOC' is an inlet of the Ionian Sea between the Greek mainland and the Peloponnese?

VP: What 'VP' is where all parallel lines in the same plane tend to meet?

CP: Which 'CP' is artificially formed by introducing an irritant into an oyster?

KH: Which 'KH' was the founder of the Independent Labour Party at the end of the 19th century?

LT	------------------	CK	------------------
LOL	------------------	AC	------------------
WH	------------------	BB	------------------
TBF	------------------	ML	------------------
SJ	------------------	AP	------------------
BOT	------------------	WAW	------------------
JK	------------------	TL	------------------
FR	------------------	TC	------------------
GB	------------------	YF	------------------
SV	------------------	VV	------------------

47

LT: Which 'LT' was the Russian revolutionary assassinated with an ice-pick?

LOL: What 'LOL' does someone live in if they have every comfort money can buy?

WH: What 'WH' is the cave near Wells in Somerset?

TBF: What 'TBF' did the black sheep have in the nursery rhyme?

SJ: Which 'SJ's biography did Boswell write?

BOT: What 'BOT' is the difference between a country's imports and exports?

JK: Which 'JK' is Captain of the Starship Enterprise?

FR: What 'FR' do primitive people perform to ensure an abundance of food and the birth of children?

GB: Which 'GB' was for many years the controversial Captain of Yorkshire Cricket Club?

SV: What 'SV' is a shy and modest person known as?

CK: What 'CK' was the film about a newspaper tycoon starring and directed by Orson Wells?

AC: What 'AC' is an international yachting trophy won every year by the same country until 1985?

BB: Which 'BB' founded the left-wing pop organisation Red Wedge?

ML: What 'ML' was an old-fashioned way of showing picture slides?

AP: Which 'AP' resigned as conductor of the Royal Philharmonic Orchestra in 1986?

WAW: What 'WAW' are terms for the increasing and decreasing of the moon?

TL: Which 'TL' is an American professor famous for his satirical songs?

TC: What 'TC' are hip-hip-hooray?

YF: What 'YF' is an infectious tropical disease characterised by jaundice?

VV: What 'VV' means the same thing is true the other way round?

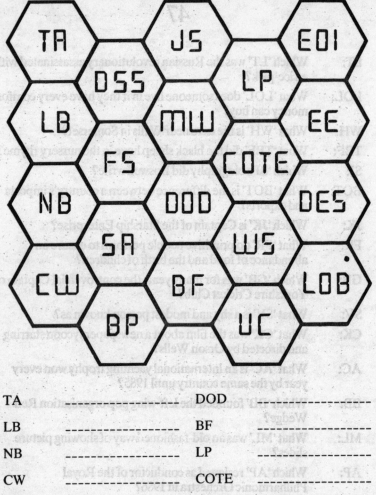

TA	---------------	DOD	---------------
LB	---------------	BF	---------------
NB	---------------	LP	---------------
CW	---------------	COTE	---------------
DSS	---------------	WS	---------------
FS	---------------	UC	---------------
SA	---------------	EOI	---------------
BP	---------------	EE	---------------
JS	---------------	DES	---------------
MW	---------------	LOB	---------------

48

TA: Which 'TA's live at Ambridge?

LB: What 'LB' do artists usually live on in Paris?

NB: To which 'NB' did Beethoven originally dedicate his Eroica Symphony?

CW: What 'CW' is a woman who is meant to be above suspicion – possibly married to Julius?

DSS: What 'DSS' starred Madonna and Rosanna Arquette?

FS: What 'FS' include sight, taste and touch?

SA: What 'SA' is the Scottish home of the Royal and Ancient Golf Club?

BP: What 'BP' do you record your vote on in an election?

JS: Which 'JS' is the ex-Bronski Beat member who now sings with the Communards?

MW: What 'MW' is a large kind of beet used as cattle food?

DOD: Which 'DOD' owns the stately home Chatsworth?

BF: What 'BF' does someone who drops a ball have?

LP: What 'LP's are Coleridge, Southey and Wordsworth?

COTE: What 'COTE' lives at Number 11 Downing Street?

WS: What 'WS' is the largest living fish – harmless to man though it may not sound it?

UC: What 'UC' is a phrase meaning living in tents or that the sails of a ship are spread?

EOI: What 'EOI' did Queen Victoria become in 1876?

EE: What 'EE' did Fabergé make jewelled versions of for Tzar Alexander III?

DES: What 'DES' is the capital of Tanzania?

LOB: What 'LOB' might you do if you are very eager to be helpful – be careful you don't fall over?

ME	-------------------	TA	-------------------
LOTL	-------------------	GKW	-------------------
TSK	-------------------	OGP	-------------------
CC	-------------------	SS	-------------------
AB	-------------------	BTF	-------------------
BV	-------------------	LJ	-------------------
BAB	-------------------	MB	-------------------
DSS	-------------------	MB	-------------------
EC	-------------------	SS	-------------------
ML	-------------------	MG	-------------------

49

ME: What 'ME' is a still active volcano in Sicily?

LOTL: What 'LOTL' is the country someone is no longer in when they are dead?

TSK: What 'TSK' was Louis XIV of France known as?

CC: What 'CC' were Dachau and Buchenwald infamous examples of?

AB: Which 'AB' wrote *The Clockwork Orange* and *Earthly Powers*?

BV: What 'BV' is a capillary?

BAB: What 'BAB' had a friend called Little Weed?

DSS: What 'DSS' are a collection of Jewish religious writings found in a cave in Israel?

EC: Which 'EC' was a Kraftwerk album released in 1986?

ML: What 'ML' is work done with the hands?

TA: Which 'TA' is the youngest woman tennis player to have won the US Open singles title?

GKW: Which 'GKW' produced heat-giving footsteps in Czechoslovakia?

OGP: What 'OGP' was Henry Fonda's last film in which he starred with his daughter and Katherine Hepburn?

SS: What 'SS' is another name for a meteor?

BTF: What 'BTF' was a satirical show of the 1950s starring Peter Cook, Dudley Moore, Jonathan Miller and Alan Bennett?

LJ: What 'LJ' did airmen know as a Mae West?

MB: Which 'MB' is the cartoonist who is editor of *Tatler*?

MB: What 'MB' is an official bearing a staff?

SS: What 'SS' can be caused by a whirlwind in a very dry area?

MG: What 'MG' is a chestnut iced with sugar?

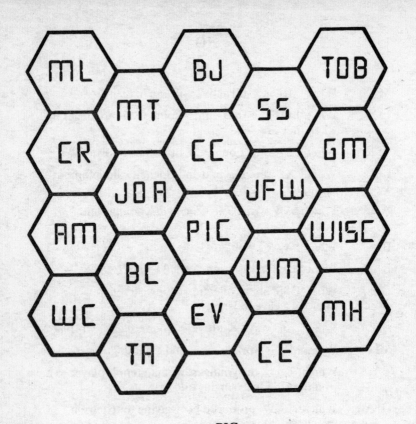

ML	----------------	PIC	----------------
CR	----------------	EV	----------------
AM	----------------	SS	----------------
WC	----------------	JFW	----------------
MT	----------------	WM	----------------
JOA	----------------	CE	----------------
BC	----------------	TOB	----------------
TA	----------------	GM	----------------
BJ	----------------	WISC	----------------
CC	----------------	MH	----------------

50

ML: What 'ML' is the emblem of Canada?

CR: What 'CR' is the Central American republic whose capital is San José?

AM: What 'AM' is the mental state of someone very vague – particularly professors?

WC: What 'WC', also known as pertussis, is an infectious respiratory disease usually caught by children?

MT: What 'MT' is famous for its Chamber of Horrors?

JOA: Which 'JOA' was also known as the Maid of Orleans?

BC: What 'BC' is another name for a pram?

TA: What 'TA' by Keats begins, 'Season of mists and mellow fruitfulness'?

BJ: Which 'BJ' is a cricket commentator and presents *Down Your Way*?

CC: Which 'CC' was Hollywood's Oriental detective?

PIC: What 'PIC' is an accomplice in illegal acts?

EV: What 'EV' are a composition by Elgar based on an unknown theme?

SS: What 'SS' are MI5 and MI6 part of?

JFW: What 'JFW' is the best-selling exercise book and video created by an American film actress?

WM: What 'WM' is the lady who looks after the costumes in a theatre?

CE: Which 'CE' married the tennis player John Lloyd?

TOB: What 'TOB' was a Biblical building full of meaningless noise?

GM: Which 'GM' was lead singer with Wham?

WISC: What 'WISC' is a bad character dressed up like an innocent one?

MH: Which 'MH', famous for his reporting of the Falklands conflict, is now editor of the *Daily Telegraph*?

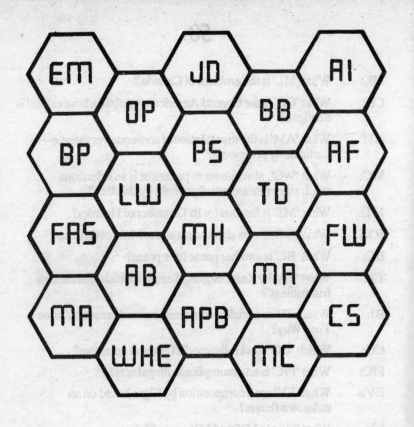

EM	------------------	MH	------------------
BP	------------------	APB	------------------
FAS	------------------	BB	------------------
MA	------------------	TD	------------------
OP	------------------	MA	------------------
LW	------------------	MC	------------------
AB	------------------	AI	------------------
WHE	------------------	AF	------------------
JD	------------------	FW	------------------
PS	------------------	CS	------------------

51

EM: Which 'EM' starred in *Beverly Hills Cop* and *48 Hours*?

BP: What 'BP' lists the aristocracy of Great Britain?

FAS: Which 'FAS' were the duo that wrote songs about a hippopotamus and other animals?

MA: What 'MA' do you do when adding up figures in your head?

OP: Which 'OP' was the Swedish Prime Minister assassinated in 1985?

LW: What 'LW' might a victor have placed on his head, but which he shouldn't rest on?

AB: What 'AB' is the name of the New Zealand rugby team?

WHE: What 'WHE' means beware of eavesdroppers – a strange architectural feature?

JD: Which 'JD's first album was *Unknown Pleasures* recorded in 1979?

PS: Which 'PS' was the name of the Yorkshire Ripper?

MH: Which 'MH' usually presents her *Pick of the Week* on Radio 4?

APB: What 'APB' is made with sheets as a joke?

BB: Which 'BB' was known as the Fat Owl of the Remove?

TD: What 'TD' is meant to be a very loving kind of bird known for its cooing?

MA: Which 'MA' is reported to have said, 'Let them eat cake'?

MC: What 'MC' has no tail and comes from the Isle of Man?

AI: What 'AI' in the South Pacific are exactly the other side of the world from London?

AF: What 'AF', written by a Greek slave, are short moral tales?

FW: What 'FW', like port or sherry, is made by the addition of brandy?

CS: What 'CS' should people have if they are going to act in a practical manner?

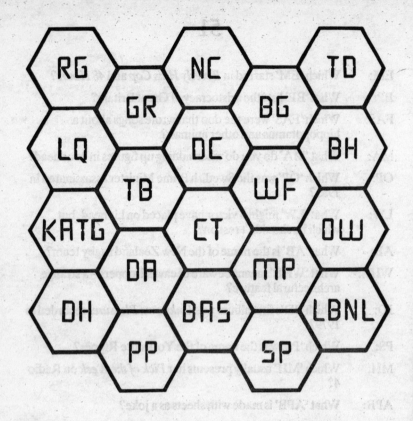

RG _____   CT _____

LQ _____   BAS _____

KATG _____   BG _____

DH _____   WF _____

GR _____   MP _____

TB _____   SP _____

DA _____   TD _____

PP _____   BH _____

NC _____   OW _____

DC _____   LBNL _____

52

RG: Which 'RG' became Prime Minister of India after his mother's assassination?

LQ: What 'LQ' is a bohemian part of a city often called?

KATG: Which 'KATG' recorded the single 'Victory' in 1986?

DH: What 'DH' is it no use flogging?

GR: Which 'GR' was Champion Jockey for 12 consecutive years?

TB: What 'TB' is the home of the Royal Shakespeare Company in London?

DA: Which 'DA' starred in *Ghostbusters* and *Trading Places*?

PP: What 'PP' does someone have if they can sing exactly in tune?

NC: Which 'NC' wrote the play *Private Lives* and the song 'Mad Dogs and Englishmen'?

DC: What 'DC' was Wyatt Earp sheriff of?

CT: Which 'CT' presented *Tiswas* and *Over The Top* on television?

BAS: What 'BAS' is a dish made of cold meat fried with chopped vegetables – it's a bit noisy?

BG: What 'BG' included Virginia Woolf, Lytton Strachey and E M Forster?

WF: What 'WF' were a famous American stagecoach company?

MP: Which 'MP' introduced pasta to Italy on his return from China?

SP: What 'SP' is a marionette?

TD: What 'TD' runs from the Black Forest to the Black Sea?

BH: What 'BH' in London is the headquarters of the Royal Academy of Arts?

OW: Which 'OW' made the first power-driven aeroplane flight?

LBNL: What 'LBNL' is at the end in occurrence, but not in importance?

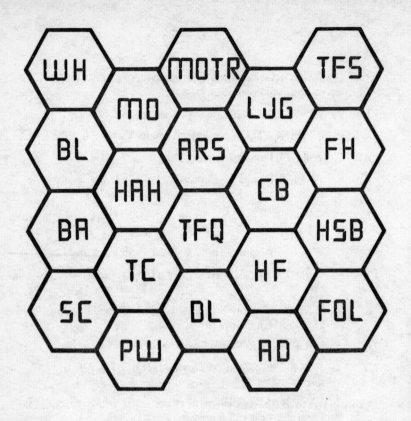

WH	------------------	TFQ	------------------
BL	------------------	DL	------------------
BA	------------------	LJG	------------------
SC	------------------	CB	------------------
MO	------------------	HF	------------------
HAH	------------------	AD	------------------
TC	------------------	TFS	------------------
PW	------------------	FH	------------------
MOTR	------------------	HSB	------------------
ARS	------------------	FOL	------------------

53

WH: What 'WH' in Berkshire traditionally commemorates Alfred's victory over the Danes?

BL: What 'BL' is abusive talk and swearing known as?

BA: What 'BA' does cyanide smell of?

SC: What 'SC' is formed by Opposition ministers?

MO: What 'MO' in cricket has no runs scored in it?

HAH: What 'HAH' might an unwelcome visitor eat you out of?

TC: Which 'TC' recorded 'You'll Never Walk Alone' in aid of the victims of the Bradford football stadium disaster?

PW: What 'PW' is also known as the coyote?

MOTR: Which 'MOTR' is Judge John Donaldson?

ARS: What 'ARS' protected civilians from bombings – particularly during the Blitz?

TFQ: Which 'TFQ' is Edmund Spenser's epic allegorical poem?

DL: What 'DL' is thought of as the heart of London's theatreland?

LJG: Which 'LJG' was queen for ten days?

CB: What 'CB' is part of the skull below the eyes?

HF: Which 'HF' starred in *Blade Runner* and *Raiders of the Lost Ark*?

AD: What 'AD' form a delta at the mouth of the river?

TFS: What 'TFS' is Vivaldi's most famous composition?

FH: What 'FH' is a packed theatre – also a winning combination in poker?

HSB: Which 'HSB' features Captain Furillo and his men on television?

FOL: What 'FOL', also known as Hanukkah, is the Jewish celebration involving special candles?

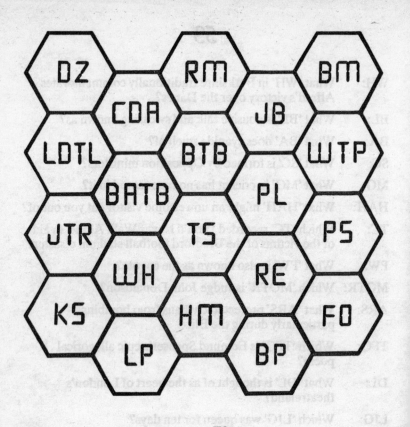

DZ	-----------------	TS	-----------------
LDTL	-----------------	HM	-----------------
JTR	-----------------	JB	-----------------
KS	-----------------	PL	-----------------
CDA	-----------------	RE	-----------------
BATB	-----------------	BN	-----------------
WH	-----------------	BM	-----------------
LP	-----------------	WTP	-----------------
RM	-----------------	PS	-----------------
BTB	-----------------	FO	-----------------

54

DZ: Which 'DZ' is Boris Pasternak's famous Russian novel?

LDTL: What 'LDTL' does someone do who speaks authoritatively, particularly if they are a judge?

JTR: Which 'JTR' terrorised Victorian London?

KS: What 'KS' did someone take if they were enlisting to become a soldier?

CDA: What 'CDA' is the South coast of France known as?

BATB: What 'BATB' does someone do if they are approaching a subject in a very roundabout way – perhaps in a garden?

WH: What 'WH' is a medicinal lotion used on cuts derived from the bark of a small tree?

LP: What 'LP' does a rocket take-off from?

RM: Which 'RM' is Prime Minister of Zimbabwe?

BTB: What 'BTB' is where someone would hit if they were fighting unfairly?

TS: What 'TS' is the most popular sporting event on US television?

HM: Which 'HM' was the famous artist particularly known for his sculptures of sheep?

JB: Which 'JB' is a female impressionist particularly famous for her portrayal of Mrs Thatcher?

PL: What 'PL' shows how far a ship may be submerged when loaded?

RE: What 'RE' is the major theatre in Manchester?

BN: What 'BN' is the most intelligent species of the dolphin family?

BM: What 'BM' was a gangster movie with an entire cast of children?

WTP: What 'WTP' might a pirate force someone to do as a punishment?

PS: Which 'PS' had a hit with 'You Can Call Me Al' from his album *Graceland*?

FO: What 'FO' is the name given to radioactive material after a nuclear explosion?

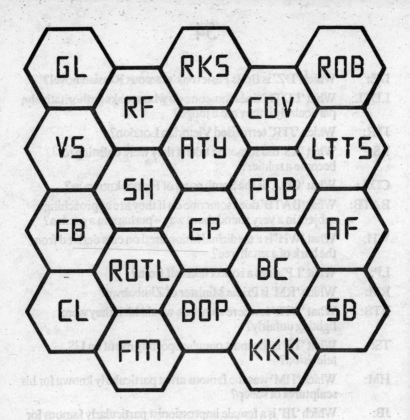

GL	------------------	EP	------------------
VS	------------------	BOP	------------------
FB	------------------	CDV	------------------
CL	------------------	FOB	------------------
RF	------------------	BC	------------------
SH	------------------	KKK	------------------
ROTL	------------------	ROB	------------------
FM	------------------	LTTS	------------------
RKS	------------------	AF	------------------
ATY	------------------	SB	------------------

55

GL: What 'GL's include Superior, Huron and Michigan?

VS: What 'VS' are a woman's bust, waist and hip measurements known as?

FB: Which 'FB' is sometimes believed to have been the author of Shakespeare's plays?

CL: What 'CL' is a thin bit of glass or plastic fitted to the eye to correct defective vision?

RF: What 'RF' is the name given to protein present in the red blood cells of 85% of people?

SH: What 'SH' is an abattoir?

ROTL: What 'ROTL' is a famous satirical poem by Alexander Pope?

FM: What 'FM' ends a game of chess with your opponent's second move?

RKS: Which 'RKS' is the ex-MP who presents *Day to Day*?

ATY: What 'ATY' is the length of a millenium?

EP: Which 'EP' had a hit with 'Memories' from the show *Cats*?

BOP: What 'BOP' was the scene of an unsuccessful invasion attempt on Cuba in 1961?

CDV: Which 'CDV' is the villainess in *One Hundred and One Dalmatians*?

FOB: What 'FOB' might you be if you are in high spirits or have just eaten a meal of pulses?

BC: Which 'BC' conquered cancer and rode to victory in the 1981 Grand National?

KKK: What 'KKK' is an American secret society?

ROB: What 'ROB' was recorded by both Chuck Berry and the Electric Light Orchestra?

LTTS: What 'LTTS' is an innocent person going to a dreadful fate?

AF: What 'AF' flies Concorde with British Airways?

SB: What 'SB' is an army officer's leather belt and straps?

Solution: Puzzle 1

BBG: Barbara Bel Geddes; DB: David Bowie; JGG: Jolly Green Giant; RB: Raymond Briggs; AS: Aegean Sea; RC: Rubber Cheque; GC: Geneva Convention; SI: Spitting Image; SC: Sistine Chapel; CB: Carte Blanche; WH: Warren Hastings; LW: Lambeth Walk; NL: Nine Lives; OD: Offa's Dyke; FAB: Flesh And Blood; ER: *Easy Rider*; RP: Rillington Place; MT: Maundy Thursday; FP: Fred Perry; WW: Wild West.

Solution: Puzzle 2

CG: California Girls; HC: Halley's Comet; SUL: Stiff Upper Lip; VC: Vatican City; ER: Egon Ronay; OV: Old Vic; NP: North Pole; WB: Wet Blanket; PC: Pontefract Castle; JT: Joseph Turner; TT: Tina Turner; TB: The Blanket; QR: Queensbury Rules; RM: Robert Maxwell; ES: Ernest Shepherd; ESB: Empire State Building; BH: Bob Hope; BM: Black Market; PH: Pearl Harbor; PP: Pat Phoenix.

Solution: Puzzle 3

JC: James Cagney; GS: General Strike; MAH: Milk And Honey; PE: Population Explosion; EM: Elgin Marbles; TB: Three Balls; AF: Aretha Franklin; TI: Terra Incognita; BB: Big Bang; OBS: Outward Bound Schools; PG: Paul Gaugin; CB: Charlie Brown; OC: Old Contemptibles; KP: Kensington Palace; FM: Frank Muir; TI: *Towering Inferno*; WM: William Morris; AHDN: *A Hard Day's Night*; GC: Grand Canyon; JL: Joe Louis.

Solution: Puzzle 4

NE: Noel Edmonds; FD: Fourth Dimension; SOK: Sport Of Kings; BM: Bob Marley; TOR: Theory of Relativity; TW: Terry Waite; FI: Fair Isle; SSB: Star Spangled Banner; LOB: *Life Of Brian*; AW: Andy Warhol; AP: Alexandra Palace; CM: Church Mouse; TU: Trade Unions; LG: Leslie Grantham; GT: Globe Theatre; PF: Pilgrim Fathers; BW: Bertie Wooster; WE: White Elephant; RM: Royal Mile; FE: First Empire.

Solution: Puzzle 5

JA: Jane Eyre; PTP: Pole to Pole; FS: Fleet Street; POG: Pot Of Gold; OB: Old Bailey; SL: Saint Leger; PC: Primary Colours; SJ: Spaghetti Junction; RC: Railway Carriage; QS: Queer Street; DV: Darth Vadar; SI: Split Infinitive; PIOT: Peace In Our Time; MP: Miss Piggy; LJS: Long John Silver; NMA: New Model Army; TOC: Two Of Clubs; OFAH: *Only Fools And Horses*; EJ: Elton John; GFOL: Great Fire Of London.

Solution: Puzzle 6

GI: Galapagos Islands; RC: Ryder Cup; MC: Marie Curie; BP: Blue Period; KE: King's Evil; TBO: Trial By Ordeal; CR: Cash Register; BB: Blues Brothers; GT: Ghost Town; BK: Bisto Kids; RC: Raymond Chandler; CP: Cinque Ports; GR: Gold Rush; MG: Mardi Gras; YAY: Yin And Yang; PMF: Pigs Might Fly; JL: John Lennon; NBN: *North By Northwest*; MG: Marvyn Gaye; GG: Golden Goose.

Solution: Puzzle 7

AH: Annie Hall; YO: Yoko Ono; KAK: Kith And Kin; WG: White Goddess; KR: King's Ransom; OH: Osborne House; GC: George Cross; EH: Emma Hamilton; AH: Achilles Heel; RR: Roland Rat; FL: Foreign Legion; BH: *Ben Hur*; LK: Lord Kitchener; UP: Uffizi Palace; GJ: Grace Jones; PL: Poet Laureate; RI: Richard Ingrams; TW: Troubled Waters; NT: New Town; ZB: Zola Budd.

Solution: Puzzle 8

AM: Adrian Mole; MD: Mary Decker; GB: Green Belt; LG: La Gioconda; BOTR: Band On The Run; FF: Forbidden Fruit; AI: Amnesty International; HG: Home Guard; ME: Mount Everest; SP: Square Peg; GG: Gretna Green; GC: Geiger Counter; BSD: Back Seat Driver; GO: Greenwich Observatory; AFOD: *A Fistful Of Dollars*; GL: Green Light; OAD: Oak Apple Day; MH: Mansion House; GF: Glyndebourne Festival; SI: Sandwich Island.

Solution: Puzzle 9

KP: Khyber Pass; DU: Down Under; SD: Salvador Dali; MW: Mae West; EF: *Emmerdale Farm*; AFTA: *A Farewell To Arms*; AE: Alter Ego; ID: Independence Day; LP: Long Parliament; CAD: Chas and Dave; GP: Gallup Poll; FH: Four Horsemen; TE: The Emmanuels; OW: Opium Wars; BH: Buddy Holly; JG: Jimmy Greaves; BD: Bottom Dollar; TPA: Tin Pan Alley; ENF: Elephants Never Forget; RB: Richard Burton.

Solution: Puzzle 10

JT: John Tenniel; BD: Bottom Drawer; SOF: Society Of Friends; AD: Anne Diamond; SA: Stella Artois; DR: Damon Runyon; OS: Ordnance Survey; PI: Pitcairn Island; NN: Never Never; BYT: Bright Young Things; NP: Nobel Prize; LF: Little Finger; HS: Haile Selassie; SBTC: Slow Boat To China; FS: Frank Sinatra; GH: George Holloway; AAC: Abbott And Costello; WF: White Flag; HK: Hara-Kiri; JT: James Thurber.

Solution: Puzzle 11

GGB: Golden Gate Bridge; KK: Kubla Khan; DB: Double Bass; LEF: Liberty, Equality, Fraternity; RR: Rat Race; ETU: Ethelred The Unready; AM: Alkali Metals; RAF: Rank And File; RB: Roger Bannister; ET: Euro-Tunnel; GD: Ghost Dance; CO: Carry On; EA: El Alamein; BA: Barbary Ape; FP: Food Poisoning; RLD: Red Letter Day; PD: Paul Daniels; PP: Party Pooper; DB: Dogger Bank; OMOV: One Man, One Vote.

Solution: Puzzle 12

AK: Ayatollah Khomeini; DI: Devil's Island; AS: April Showers; FAE: *First Among Equals*; RA: Ron Atkinson; SAD: Stand And Deliver; GFAM: Gold, Frankincense And Myrrh; OFS: Orange Free State; SV: Silicone Valley; TJ: Traffic Jams; LHO: Lee Harvey Oswald; AN: Assumed Name; SNF: *Saturday Night Fever*; PF: Paddy Field; TL: Tea Leaf; AC: Alimentary Canal; SAA: Sackcloth And Ashes; MJ: Mick Jagger; BD: *Blind Date*; DP: Doberman Pinscher.

Solution: Puzzle 13

WOG: Winter Olympic Games; GC: Giant's Causeway; LG: Laughing Gas; TAS: Trouble And Strife; LW: Lot's Wife; GSFM: Great Step For Mankind; OTL: Over The Limit; TRF: The Red Flag; MD: Moby Dick; WOTE: Whites Of Their Eyes; LOO: Land Of Opportunity; VVG: Vincent Van Gogh; KTK: Kiri Te Kanawa; DR: Divine Right; LAG: Loving And Giving; RR: Ronald Reagan; CPR: Canadian Pacific Railway; ITB: In The Beginning; CP: Cleft Palate; BTTW: Backs To The Wall.

Solution: Puzzle 14

AW: A Week; NS: Nova Scotia; TOT: Trick Or Treat; BR: Boat Race; NL: New Leaf; GM: Gila Monster; BT: Brass Tacks; FF: Five Farthings; TP: The Pentagon; JW: John Wayne; SD: Steve Davis; MM: Memento Mori; AOR: Age Of Reason; NO: Noblesse Oblige; HE: Her Indoors; WC: White City; SW: Still Waters; HH: Heinrich Himmler; DN: Deadly Nightshade; MIH: Marry In Haste.

Solution: Puzzle 15

CN: Cleopatra's Needle; DAAL: Drunk As A Lord; GM: Glen Miller; PROC: People's Republic Of China; OTM: Over The Moon; GB: Gall Bladder; TYO: *The Young Ones*; CDS: Cul De Sac; CO: Clapham Omnibus; SOI: Shah Of Iran; SP: Shetland Pony; SB: Sarah Brightman; FH: Free House; WEJ: W E Johns; DN: *Doctor No*; KOD: Kiss Of Death; HA: Heart Attack; PF: Photo-Finish; DB: Domesday Book; LB: London Bridge.

Solution: Puzzle 16

SL: Simon LeBon; BW: Boogie Woogie; LOTL: Lady Of The Lake; OM: Old Maid; MS: Mike Smith; COR: Colossus Of Rhodes; SD: Stable Door; BN: Beaujolais Nouveau; AS: Apron Strings; AB: Aurora Borealis; CR: *Casino Royale*; CLO: Cod Liver Oil; SB: Simon Bolivar; RT: Red Tape; BS: Black Sea; GG: Germaine Greer; BOE: Bank Of England; TAN: Tooth And Nail; CP: Catherine Parr; IC: Iron Curtain.

Solution: Puzzle 17

MP: Michael Parkinson; BS: Black Sheep; OP: Opium Poppy; US: Uncle Sam; BG: Bob Geldolf; CR: Cock Robin; BS: Bosporus Strait; IS: Indian Summer; PT: Pete Townsend; CL: Calf Love; BT: Bolshoi Theatre; CS: Cocker Spaniel; BW: Blue Whale; HJ: Hattie Jacques; OST: Old School Tie; SF: Sinn Fein; CC: Catherine Cookson; JC: Juvenile Courts; SAN: Straight And Narrow; EIC: East India Company.

Solution: Puzzle 18

RB: Richard Branson; EB: Early Bird; GF: Golden Fleece; FM: Freddie Mercury; SOL: Statue Of Liberty; BB: Buffalo Bill; BP: Beatrix Potter; SYI: *Seven Year Itch*; TCP: *The Color Purple*; ML: Missing Link; BL: Bodleian Library; LB: Lizzie Borden; CB: Camel's Back; ET: Eiffel Tower; EW: Evelyn Waugh; SG: Sir Galahad; TMS: *The Magnificent Seven*; DE: Doppler Effect; RR: Red Rag; JJ: Jesse James.

Solution: Puzzle 19

GW: Gallic Wars; CB: Collar Bone; PC: Phil Collins; EC: Elephant's Child; JJ: Ju-Jitsu; DAJ: Darby And Joan; CI: Channel Islands; BM: Bloody Mary; CS: Cold Shoulder; JP: Jet Propulsion; FW: Fatima Whitbread; LS: Leopard's Spots; DS: Dead Sea; HMD: Hand-Me-Downs; FB: *First Blood*; JC: Jackie Collins; SC: Sweet Chariot; BT: Bo Tree; DJ: Derek Jameson; LL: Lapis Lazuli.

Solution: Puzzle 20

OATH: Old As The Hills; UD: Ugly Duckling; COF: *Chariots of Fire*; GEM: Green Eyed Monster; LM: Little Mermaid; CE: Curate's Egg; WOJ: Walls Of Jericho; LB: Little Bear; BTP: Boston Tea Party; AL: Aladdin's Lamp; KA: Kingsley Amis; MU: Midge Ure; WO: Wild Oats; CC: Common Cold; JB: Jodrell Bank; WB: Whipping Boy; LH: Lloyd Honeyghan; LD: Les Dawson; GF: Green Fingers; WS: Weird Sisters.

Solution: Puzzle 21

MW: Michael Wood; OFS: One For Sorrow; MF: Mickey Finn; FBT: Fun Boy Three; WF: White Feather; MA: Mount Ararat; BF: Black Forest; GS: Galley Slave; MI: Merchant/Ivory; YF: Yellow Flag; MB: Matt Busby; BP: Barge-Pole; HK: Helmut Kohl; SDS: Seven Deadly Sins; NS: Nevil Shute; BF: Buck's Fizz; AH: Anne Hathaway; MB: Mills Bomb; SBDM: St Bartholomew's Day Massacre; AW: Artesian Well.

Solution: Puzzle 22

PC: Plaid Cymru; HC: Habeas Corpus; GR: Ginger Rogers; AAG: Ack-Ack Gun; OTC: On The Cards; YK: Yom Kippur; CS: Charge Sheet; WS: Watling Street; RAR: Romulus And Remus; BG: Bethnal Green; CD: Carl Davies; GM: German Measles; BS: Beaufort Scale; TMC: Too Many Cooks; MOK: 'Mull Of Kintyre'; MS: Maiden Speech; CS: Charlie Spedding; RBG: Royal Botanic Gardens; STR: Spare The Rod; HHM: Hector Hugh Monro.

Solution: Puzzle 23

MC: Mortal Combat; TVQ: The Virgin Queen; RT: Roget's Thesaurus; PAT: Pyramus And Thisbe; AA: Ascorbic Acid; CM: Chain Mail; AR: Aaron's Rod; LA: Louis Armstrong; BA: Buzz Aldrin; BTH: Bury The Hatchet; AC: Atlantic Cable; RR: Richard Rogers; CS: Card-Sharp; MB: Menachem Begin; SS: Set Square; DH: Dusty Hare; CS: Captain Sensible; DLL: Daddy-Long-Legs; IP: Iberian Peninsula; JT: Jacques Tati.

Solution: Puzzle 24

BH: Beverly Hills; WM: White Magic; JN: Jack Nicklaus; JW: Jay-Walker; MB: Montgolfier Brothers; SOS: Stone Of Scone; TOL: Tower Of London; MM: Moors Murders; DT: Delirium Tremens; SOD: Star Of David; LD: Lake District; SE: Sheena Easton; SBNH: Seen But Not Heard; RA: Robert Altman; AA: Adam's Apple; VDL: Van Dieman's Land; DT: Dylan Thomas; RA: Royal Assent; MG: Martha Graham; CM: Chamber Music.

Solution: Puzzle 25

FHS: Faster, Higher, Stronger; AW: Appian Way; DOJ: Day Of Judgement; MT: Mother Tongue; RS: Rood Screen; AN: Arabian Nights; ALS: Auld Lang Syne; MO: Mail Order; ZM: *Zenyatta Mondata*; QU: Queen's University; BITH: Bird In The Hand; NV: *National Velvet*; SA: Spiro Agnew; DN: Deadly Nightshade; FT: Fellow-Traveller; MB: *Madame Butterfly*; BV: Blank Verse; LW: Last Word; CF: Centrifugal Force; TW: The Wash.

Solution: Puzzle 26

MP: Mystery Plays; QOS: Queen Of Spades; LR: Little Rock; FT: Fluorescent Tube; TB: Taste Buds; PW: Peter Wright; MDM: Mal-De-Mer; LOH: Labours Of Hercules; DBH: Doctor Barnardo Homes; CC: Cassius Clay; WOH: Word Of Honour; PSB: Pet Shop Boys; DH: Dower House; OS: Open Sesame; AAH: Abelard and Heloise; SS: Sylvester Stallone; SP: Silk Purse; SIT: Stitch In Time; CP: Car Phones; JSB: Johann Sebastian Bach.

Solution: Puzzle 27

LHA: Lord High Admiral; SJ: Scott Joplin; CW: Catherine Wheel; AS: Adriatic Sea; BOA: Bard Of Avon; HW: Harry Webb; JB: Jonah Barrington; PS: Prodigal Son; VSW: Vita Sackville-West; TC: Ten Commandments; WG: Worzel Gummidge; FA: Frederick Ashton; CDM: Creme De Menthe; RB: Roger Bacon; MS: Mackerel Sky; BE: Bald Eagle; AM: Assay Mark; AD: Action Directe; SH: Saint Helena; FAM: Foot And Mouth.

Solution: Puzzle 28

GM: Graham McPherson; ASD: All Saints' Day; MQ: Mary Quant; SR: Stamford Raffles; JOAT: Jack Of All Trades; DL: Davy Lamp; YM: *Yes Minister*; CC: Cat's Cradle; SB: Sarah Bernhardt; HP: Humble Pie; TAH: Theseus And Hippolyta; EC: Entente Cordiale: FR: Fastnet Race; MC: Morse Code; CB: Charles Babbage; BG: Beat Generation; AA: Addis Ababa; BOAF: Birds Of A Feather; CT: Canine Teeth; LW: Lech Walesa.

Solution: Puzzle 29

HY: Hundred Years'; CDF: Chemin De Fer; HT: Half-Timbered; CT: Cocteau Twins; IB: Ian Botham; SS: Sister Ship; AYM: Angry Young Men; MLK: Martin Luther King; JW: Johnny Weismuller; STT: Sabre-Toothed Tiger; BMN: Beggar My Neighbour; LSDL: Let Sleeping Dogs Lie; PA: Pallas Athene; TG: Tear Gas; BI: Baffin Island; AR: Artificial Respiration; JB: Jerry Built; WCOD: White Cliffs Of Dover; RA: Riot Act; KI: Kharg Island.

Solution: Puzzle 30

NT: Norman Tebbit; DC: Dutch Courage; SS: Seven Sacraments; GA: Gerry Anderson; PI: Percussion Instruments; FP: Freezing Point; FZ: Franco Zefferelli; DOW: Duke Of Wellington; VR: Von Ribbentrop; HB: Handle-Bar; SOS: Swing Out Sister; WL: Wagon Lit; LC: Low Countries; BHT: Badminton Horse Trials; SOD: Sword Of Damocles; LA: Local Anaesthetic; JP: Jack Pot; IA: Isaac Asimov; PR: Proportional Representation; LAY: Lancaster And York.

Solution: Puzzle 31

SR: Square Root; GOS: Great Ormond Street; WFG: *Waiting For Godot*; MW: Milky Way; SE: Shining Example; WA: White Army; BG: British Gas; MG: Mike Gibson; SL: Saint Lawrence; MGR: Merry-Go-Round; EOC: Equal Opportunities Commission; DM: Douglas MacArthur; CF: Chicken Feed; FR: *Fraggle Rock*; AS: Abominable Snowman; BF: Bull Fighters; SATB: Siouxie And The Banshees; JP: John Peel; SP: Samuel Pepys; WOE: White Of Egg.

Solution: Puzzle 32

BP: Blood Poisoning; BT: Betsy Trotwood; HO: Hair Oil; BBT: Big Bang Theory; UW: Unknown Warriors; MC: Michael Crawford; JB: Jail-Bird; WAD: Wattle-And-Daub; DOL: Duchy Of Lancaster; KB: Kit-Bag; WH: *Wuthering Heights*; WJ: Wandering Jew; DP: Dennis Potter; AS: Anglo-Saxons; NT: Nuremberg Trials; CB: Cecil Beaton; WA: Westminster Abbey; JG: Joel Garner; AAL: At Arms' Length; AD: Abu Dhabi.

Solution: Puzzle 33

NS: Natural Selection; BA: Bronze Age; GC: Gate-Crasher; EOJ: Emperor Of Japan; BT: Bayeaux Tapestry; AT: Archbishop Tutu; DC: Dark Continent; BRG: Bradshaw's Railway Guide; FGTH: Frankie Goes To Hollywood; SO: Seville Orange; JF: Joe Frazier; UC: Upper Case; SC: Sean Connery; HAS: Hammer And Sickle; SBS: South Bank Show; SEF: Saint Elmo's Fire; FT: Fortune-Tellers; CC: Cheshire Cat; AV: Authorised Version; BOT: Berwick-On-Tweed.

Solution: Puzzle 34

SA: Spanish Armada; HAH: Hare And Hounds; PPR: Peter Paul Rubens; CG: Chain-Gang; JI: Jeremy Irons; FW: False Witness; CG: Colonel Gaddafi; THT: The Heavenly Twins; LB: Lumiere Brothers; DD: Dare-Devil; TE: Total Eclipse; COC: College of Cardinals; MR: Mount Rushmore; SIG: Silence Is Golden; AB: Arnold Bennett; SDA: Seventh Day Adventists; TM: Trevor McDonald; GGG: Going, Going, Gone; RB: Red Baron; MC: Molotov Cocktail.

Solution: Puzzle 35

LN: Loch Ness; GB: Green Baize; WS: Wallis Simpson; TA: The Ashes; MS: Morning Star; CAB: Cap And Bells; BOB: Battle Of Bosworth; HOL: House Of Lords; MC: Mexico City; CP: Child's Play; FM: Flora MacDonald; AA: Academy Award; MLF: Morgan Le Fay; NA: Nancy Astor; OOV: Oil Of Vitriol; WAW: Warp And Weft; FC: Face Cards; GH: Gloria Hunniford; RR: Robert Runcie; SOTF: Sit On The Fence.

Solution: Puzzle 36

FOA: Forest Of Arden; PMU: Pick-Me-Up; JA: Jeffrey Archer; CN: Cosa Nostra; DIC: Doric, Ionic, Corinthian; ROT: Reign Of Terror; VAV: Vol-Au-Vent; KMH: Kiss Me Hardy; CTC: Chewing The Cud; MA: Michael Aspel; CAA: Cain And Abel; CM: Carbon Monoxide; EH: Egg-Head; TM: Taj Mahal; MS: Magellan Strait; BOB: Baron Of Beef; GL: Gary Lineker; TR: The Ridings; KT: Knights Templar; TMM: The Merry Monarch.

Solution: Puzzle 37

AF: Athlete's Foot; NSA: New Stone Age; NO: Number One; RTB: Robert The Bruce; RB: Rule Britannia; PR: Prince Rainier; SFS: Sixty-Four-Squares; YJ: Yellow Jersey; POW: Prince Of Wales; AS: Arthur Scargill; SVD: St Vitus's Dance; WA: Woody Allen; FYP: Five Year Plan; AZ: Absolute Zero; ET: Enfant Terrible; AOTA: Acts Of The Apostles; CI: Christopher Isherwood; FOF: Figure Of Fun: KMK: *Kiss Me Kate*; CS: Caste System.

Solution: Puzzle 38

LR: Lord Reith; WS: Wall Street; STB: Sir Toby Belch; CITA: Castles In The Air; DM: *Daily Mail*; CR: Cod's Roe; GS: German Shepherd; CS: Close Shave; BA: Bikini Atoll; NNL: Never-Never Land; ML: Martin Luther; LP: Litmus Paper; SAE: Stand At Ease; VFT: Venus Fly Trap; GT: Globe-Trotter; TR: Third Reich; SP: Salisbury Plain; KM: King Minos; BS: Basque Separatists; MS: Meryl Streep.

Solution: Puzzle 39

QOTM: Queen Of The May; BS: Binary Scale; TR: *Two Ronnies*; TD: Thumbs Down; HAB: Hinge And Brackett; HH: Ha-Ha; EW: Eddie Waring; IH: Iron Hand; IA: Idi Amin; MP: Mary Poppins; POH: Pillars Of Hercules; MG: Minstrels' Gallery; AGB: Alexander Graham Bell; BG: Blood Groups; WSS: *West Side Story*; ID: Infra Dig; WE: Wall Eye; DPC: Damp-Proof Course; HS: Heysel Stadium; CONT: Cat-O'-Nine-Tails.

Solution: Puzzle 40

RCMP: Royal Canadian Mounted Police; PW: Perkin Warbeck; WOTW: Will O' The Wisp; EP: Elementary Particles; SB: Saint Bernard; SOT: Seige Of Troy; NE: Near East; HW: Hadrian's Wall; HI: Holy Innocents; CD: Camp David; EC: Estate Car; SAN: *Sid And Nancy*; WH: Wart Hog; RC: Radio-Carbon; DJL: Davy Jones' Lockers; VW: Virginia Wade; DL: Dalai Lama; BC: Belgian Congo; SS: Sob-Sister; IR: Inland Revenue.

Solution: Puzzle 41

FAJ: Flotsam And Jetsam; CH: Cotswold Hills; AOG: Act Of God; TRR: The Real Roxanne; CO: Conscientious Objectors; BM: Bader Meinhof; SOF: Soldier Of Fortune; WD: White Dwarf; SD: Stockton-Darlington; BB: Boris Becker; BRB: Back-Room Boys; EGA: Elizabeth Garrett Anderson; MR: Marathon Race; WDLM: Walter De La Mare; PW: Punkah Walla; JT: John Timpson; MM: Morris Men; HP: Harold Pinter; LD: Lame Ducks; HS: *High Society*.

Solution: Puzzle 42

CAT: Copper And Tin; WF: Wage Freeze; TS: Tristram Shandy; CC: Charlotte Corday; MO: Marching Orders; BW: Brian Wilde; OC: Oedipus Complex; PS: Peter Shilton; MMW: Mark My Words; WW: Wailing Wall; LD: Labrador Dog; BJ: Billy Joel; BOB: Battle Of Britain; CC: Charlie Chaplin; AP: Atmospheric Pressure; FL: Freddie Laker; LM: Ladies' Man; TR: *The Rivals*; EP: Edith Piaf; IC: Indian Corn.

Solution: Puzzle 43

MT: Maggie Tulliver; CE: Comprehensive Schools; MH: Music Hall; BC: Birth Control; CS: China Shop; DS: Dave Stewart; JC: Jacques Cousteau; DOE: Duke Of Edinburgh; MK: Mercy Killing; CD: Continental Drift; LT: Lambs' Tails; ML: Maginot Line; BH: Bell Hop; FT: *Fawlty Towers*; MS: Michelin Stars; AC: Agatha Christie; LIW: Lady-In-Waiting; GPB: *Gentlemen Prefer Blondes*; HU: Harvard University; JM: John McEnroe.

Solution: Puzzle 44

MC: Magna Carta; AC: Advent Calendar; SQ: Status Quo; RM: Rocky Marciano; PN: Pound Note; BTM: Before The Mast; EB: Elizabeth Bennett; HA: Hearing Aids; CR: Coral Reef; VB: Venetian Blinds; JC: James Cook; LP: Lambeth Palace; JSF: *Jeux Sans Frontières*; CC: Cheese-Cloth; PM: *Paper Moon*; FR: French Resistance; RC: Ring Cycle; LDD: La-Di-Da; EH: Emlyn Hughes; MO: Mouth Organ.

Solution: Puzzle 45

CR: Cosmic Rays; BOB: Beast Of Burden; TC: Thomas Cook; CR: Cultural Revolution; WC: Winston Churchill; BL: Bee-Line; RAG: Rosencrantz And Guildenstern; SS: Summer Solstice; BN: Barry Norman; DW: Death Watch; MC: Main Chance; TR: Tom Robinson; BY: Brewers' Yeast; NM: Nigel Mansell; PC: Percussion Caps; MM: Mad Max; HW: Hard Water; OTJ: Ode To Joy; LOL: Labour Of Love; FC: Fidel Castro.

Solution: Puzzle 46

JP: Jenny Pitman; LL: Land-Locked; AM: Alasdair Milne; MS: Military Service; JD: Jerry Dammers; ST: Sub-Titles; SLIH: *Some Like It Hot*; LG: Landscape Gardener; TPS: The Planets Suite; AI: Ad Infinitum; RH: Rolf Harris; CP: Crystal Palace; PH: Prince Hal; CP: Chelsea Pensioner; KC: King Canute; DO: Delphic Oracle; GOC: Gulf Of Corinth; VP: Vanishing Point; CP: Cultured Pearl; KH: Keir Hardie.

Solution: Puzzle 47

LT: Leon Trotsky; LOL: Lap Of Luxury; WH: Wookey Hole; TBF: Three Bags Full; SJ: Samuel Johnson; BOT: Balance Of Trade; JK: James Kirk; FR: Fertility Rites; GB: Geoff Boycott; SV: Shrinking Violet; CK: *Citizen Kane*; AC: Americas Cup; BB: Billy Bragg; ML: Magic Lantern; AP: Andre Previn; WAW: Waxing And Waning; TL: Tom Lehrer; TC: Three Cheers; YF: Yellow Fever; VV: Vice Versa.

Solution: Puzzle 48

TA: *The Archers*; LB: Left Bank; NB; Napoleon Bonaparte; CW: Caesar's Wife; DSS: *Desperately Seeking Susan*; FS: Five Senses; SA: Saint Andrews; BP: Ballot Paper; JS: Jimmy Somerville; MW: Mangel-Wurzel; DOD: Duke Of Devonshire; BF: Butter-Fingers; LP: Lake Poets; COTE: Chancellor Of The Exchequer; WS: Whale Shark; UC: Under Canvas; EOI: Empress Of India; EE: Easter Eggs; DES: Dae-Es-Salaam; LOB: Lean Over Backwards.

Solution: Puzzle 49

ME: Mount Etna; LOTL: Land Of The Living; TSK: The Sun King; CC: Concentration Camps; AB: Anthony Burgess; BV: Blood Vessel; BAB: Bill And Ben; DSS: Dead Sea Scrolls; EC: Electric Café; ML: Manual Labour; TA: Tracy Austin; GKW: Good King Wenceslas; OGP: *On Golden Pond*; SS: Shooting Star; BTF: Beyond The Fringe; LJ: Life-Jacket; MB: Marc Boxer; MB: Mace-Bearer; SS: Sand Storm; MG: Marron Glacé.

Solution: Puzzle 50

ML: Maple Leaf; CR: Costa Rica; AM: Absent Minded; WC: Whooping Cough; MT: Madame Tussauds; JOA: Joan Of Arc; BC: Baby Carriage; TA: To Autumn; BJ: Brian Johnston; CC: Charlie Chan; PIC: Partner In Crime; EV: Enigma Variations; SS: Secret Service; JFW: *Jane Fonda's Workout*; WM: Wardrobe Mistress; CE: Chris Evert; TOB: Tower Of Babel; GM: George Michael; WISC: Wolf In Sheep's Clothing; MH: Max Hastings.

Solution: Puzzle 51

EM: Eddie Murphy; BP: Burke's Peerage; FAS: Flanders And Swann; MA: Mental Arithmetic; OP: Olav Palme; LW: Laurel Wreath; AB: All Blacks; WHE: Walls Have Ears; JD: Joy Division; PS: Peter Sutcliffe; MH: Margaret Howard; APB: Apple-Pie Bed; BB: Billy Bunter; TD: Turtle Doves; MA: Marie Antoinette; MC: Manx Cat; AI: Antipodes Islands; AF: Aesop's Fables; FW: Fortified Wine; CS: Common Sense.

Solution: Puzzle 52

RG: Rajiv Gandhi; LQ: Latin Quarter; KATG: Kool And The Gang; DH: Dead Horse; GR: Gordon Richards; TB: The Barbican; DA: Dan Ackroyd; PP: Perfect Pitch; NC: Noel Coward; DC: Dodge City; CT: Chris Tarrant; BAS: Bubble And Squeak; BG: Bloomsbury Group; WF: Wells-Fargo; MP: Marco Polo; SP: String Puppet; TD: The Danube; BH: Burlington House; OW: Orville Wright; LBNL: Last But Not Least.

Solution: Puzzle 53

WH: White Horse; BL: Bad Language; BA: Bitter Almonds; SC: Shadow Cabinet; MO: Maiden Over; HAH: House And Home; TC: The Crowd; PW: Prairie Wolf; MOTR: Master Of The Rolls; ARS: Air-Raid Shelters; TFQ: The Fairie Queen; DL: Drury Lane; LJG: Lady Jane Grey; CB: Cheek-Bone; HF: Harrison Ford; AD: Alluvial Deposits; TFS: The Four Seasons; FH: Full House; HSB: *Hill Street Blues*; FOL: Festival Of Lights.

Solution: Puzzle 54

DZ: *Doctor Zhivago*; LDTL: Lay Down The Law; JTR: Jack The Ripper; KS: King's Shilling; CDA: Cote D'Azur; BATB: Beat Around The Bush; WH: Witch Hazel; LP: Launching Pad; RM: Robert Mugabe; BTB: Below The Belt; TS: The Superbowl; HM: Henry Moore; JB: Janet Brown; PL: Plimsoll Line; RE: Royal Exchange; BN: Bottle-Nosed; BM: *Bugsy Malone*; WTP: Walk The Plank; PS: Paul Simon; FO: Fall-Out.

Solution: Puzzle 55

GL: Great Lakes; VS: Vital Statistics; FB: Francis Bacon; CL: Contact Lens; RF: Rhesus Factor; SH: Slaughter House; ROTL: Rape Of The Lock; FM: Fool's Mate; RKS: Robert Kilroy-Silk; ATY: A Thousand Years; EP: Elaine Paige; BOP: Bay Of Pigs; CDV: Cruella De Ville; FOB: Full Of Beans; BC: Bob Champion; KKK: Klu Klux Klan; ROB: Roll Over Beethoven; LTTS: Lamb To The Slaughter; AF: Air France; SB: Sam Browne.